Mindfulness Most Effective Techniques

A Hands-on Approach to Reduce Stress, Stay Focused and Find Peace in the Everyday

Katherine Hofstadter

Table of Contents

Introduction

If you're reading this book, you're probably wondering why meditation studios, classes, and podcasts are starting to emerge all around you. Meditation and mindfulness are becoming quite the trend in modern-day society. Due to our increasingly stressful lives – meditation and mindfulness have never been more necessary. Maybe that's what brought you to this book in the first place! Without further ado, let's dive in.

Who Is This Book for?

This book is for anyone who wants to understand mindfulness and meditation on a deeper level, learn about the relationship between mindfulness and meditation, and begin practicing them in their daily life. This book is also for anyone who wants to learn the techniques and tips to make mindfulness a part of their daily life. If you are someone who wants to benefit from all of the tremendous positive changes that meditation will bring into your life, this book is for you! This book is for anyone, regardless of your experience with mindfulness. Whether you are a seasoned meditator or a complete beginner, there is something for you in this book!

What Will You Learn in This Book?

In this book, you will learn everything you need to know about mindfulness, and it will be taught to you with a practical approach. This means that you will be able to practice what you are learning and see real examples of how you can incorporate it into your life. This book is filled with techniques to help you begin to meditate and be mindful in your daily life. If you are an experienced meditator, this book will provide you with a quick reference guide that you can turn to anytime you need a little bit of guidance.

Mindfulness is a difficult state to achieve in your daily life, but you will become more mindful with the help of this book than you have ever been before.

What is Meditation?

Simply put, meditation is a practice where a person uses a technique, like mindfulness - to focus their thoughts and mind on an activity, thought, or object to train their awareness and attention. The goal of this is to help the person achieve clear-headedness and an emotionally calm and stable state.

What is Mindfulness?

The most popular reason people decide to learn meditation is to achieve mindfulness to combat mental obstacles. The simplest methods of meditation all surround achieving mindfulness- but what is mindfulness?

Simply put, mindfulness is a state of mind that is non-judgmental, and that frees your mind to accept everybody and everything just as it is. Mindfulness is simply an awareness practice that you use to bring your mind away from thoughts that are not of the present moment. It can also be a type of meditation used as a mental training practice that requires you to focus your mind on your thoughts and sensations in the present moment. Your thoughts include your physical sensations, passing thoughts, and current emotions.

Mindfulness meditation often utilizes mental imagery, breathing practice, muscle and body relaxation, and awareness of your mind and body.

You can achieve mindfulness through some forms of meditation, or you can simply just practice the act of it daily. You will learn how to practice both of these techniques throughout this book.

The Relationship Between Mindfulness and Meditation

The relationship between mindfulness and meditation is an important one. Mindfulness can be practiced in any form, not just meditation. However, meditation is a great exercise to help a person facilitate mindfulness if they have never practiced it before. Experienced meditators can practice mindfulness without the use of a session of meditation. However, for beginners who are just learning about mindfulness, learning about different meditation types that can facilitate mindfulness will be important in their learning process.

In this book, I will be teaching you about five different types of meditation. All of these meditations will help you practice mindfulness. In addition, simply just learning these meditations will help you see that different types of meditations can help offer a different aspect of mindfulness. By understanding this, you will be able to choose the ideal meditation type for you to practice based on your set of needs.

A Brief History of Meditation

So, you might be wondering where meditation and mindfulness came from and how they have become so relevant in today's societies. In this section, I will provide you with a brief history of meditation.

The first written evidence of meditation was first seen in the Vedas in 1500 BCE. The Vedas are a collection of ancient religious texts and hymns written in India between 1500 and 1000 BCE. This means that meditation was first developed in India.

In India, there is a tradition of *Guru and Shishya,* which is the modern-day equivalent of teacher and disciple. Students of this tradition were sent to schools that were located in forests to learn and live under a successful teacher. During this time, all of the learning and knowledge on this topic were passed on through word of mouth.

In almost all Hindu religious books, meditation was written about in some form or another. Due to this fact, we can assume that meditation was an integral part of the knowledge that the Gurus were teaching their disciples - and this was all done through oral tradition. We can all safely assume then that if most of the early meditation was done through word of mouth, it could mean that the practice of meditation actually dates back to a time before 1500 BCE, which was the first written document of meditation.

Meditation has changed over the last thousands of years and is much more accessible than it was in its infancy. Anyone can begin to practice mediation in this day and age; all you need is some time and a smartphone application. This means that you do not need to travel and train to become a Buddhist monk to benefit from mindfulness and meditation. All you need is 10 minutes per day and some dedication! There is no magic and no secret. The benefits of mindfulness are proven by science, and you can harness them by simply showing up every day!

Chapter 1: Why Should You Meditate?

Meditation has changed over the last thousands of years into something that everyone can do comfortably in their own homes. Nowadays, meditation is more easily accessible, and you don't necessarily need your own Guru to learn it. In this chapter, we will look at some of the many benefits of meditation.

The Benefits of Meditation

The benefits of meditation begin with improving your mental health, which then helps improve your physical health as well. In this section, I will discuss the ten most common benefits of meditation.

Meditation Reduces Stress

Benefit number one; Stress reduction. This is the most common ailment that people decide to pick up meditation for. A recent study of 3,500 adults showed that meditation did, in fact, live up to its reputation for reducing stress. Stress, whether it be mental or physical, is caused by the increased *cortisol* levels, which is a stress hormone in our bodies. It is responsible for all the unhealthy symptoms of stress. These symptoms can range from sleep disruption all the way to depression and anxiety, and in some cases, increased blood pressure. It is also a regular contributor to overall fatigue and foggy thinking. Meditation helps battle stress effectively because being mindful is stress' kryptonite. Naturally, when humans are in a state of stress, our minds start to go crazy. We begin thinking of all the worst-case scenarios and how that would lead to our untimely demise.

Let's use Josephine as an example. Josephine works in a lawyers' office as a paralegal and is constantly under a lot of stress. She forgot to submit a document to her boss, which had a deadline of three hours ago. Naturally, Josephine's mind goes wild - "My boss is going to be so angry! They are going to sit me down and fire me. I just signed a lease to my new apartment; I can't afford to lose this job! I'm going to have to sell my car and move back in with my parents after this! But I hate living with my parents - they are going to drive me insane. I'll become so depressed and etc. etc. etc." This is where mindfulness comes into play. Instead of spiraling at the thought of the mistake she made at work; she is able to focus on the task at hand. She would be able to reason with herself and think, "Why am I so scared and stressed?" and be able to answer her own thoughts. Being able to be reasonable with your own thoughts actually prevents the spiraling, which in turn reduces stress. With mindfulness, Josephine can now say to herself, "Well, I've done a great job in the last year at this job - I don't think my boss will fire me over one missed document. I better go tell them now and submit the document that I've missed." This is the reasonable response that we all want to have in our head whenever something goes wrong in our lives. Meditation and the practice of mindfulness will be able to help people with that.

Meditation Reduces Anxiety

Benefit number two; controlling and reducing anxiety. Stress and anxiety are partners in crime. One tends to lead to another and vice versa. Overall, having less stress, in general, tends to lead to less anxiety.

In a recent study, people participated in an eight-week trial of mindfulness meditation in hopes of reducing their anxiety. The study showed that mindfulness helped reduce serious symptoms of chronic anxiety such as; OCD, panic attacks, phobias, paranoia, and social anxiety.

Three years later, another study followed up with the same group of volunteers after they completed the 8-week mindfulness meditation trial. More than half of the volunteers had continued to practice regular meditation and achieved lower anxiety levels in their day to day lives. Many of those participants have begun practicing meditation in other forms, such as yoga.

Yoga is a form of meditation that has scientifically been proven to help people reduce anxiety. This is caused by the benefits of physical exercise and meditation together.

Meditation in any form should be a must in the lives of people who work in high-pressure work environments. Job-related anxiety is one of the leading causes of anxiety in today's society. Meditation is a safe and proven way to combat the daily stressors of a demanding and emotionally taxing job.

Meditation Increases Your Emotional Wellbeing

Meditation promotes better emotional health and wellbeing. Similar to how stress and anxiety are partners in crime - emotional health is the overall state of your mind.

Lowering negative emotions such as stress and anxiety leaves room in your mind for more positive emotions such as happiness and calmness. There are forms of meditation out there that can help a person lead to a better self-image and build a life in a more positive light.

In the same study discussed above, those who meditated experienced long term decreases in depression and better overall emotional health. A few other scientific studies suggest that meditation can treat depression by decreasing cytokines. Cytokines are inflammatory chemicals in your brain that are released in response to stress, which negatively affects a person's mood and can lead to depression in the long run.

Meditation Fosters Kindness

Meditation helps generate kindness. As mentioned briefly above, mindfulness and self-awareness generate compassion and sympathy, which fall under the umbrella trait of kindness.

Some types of meditation actually focus more on increasing positive actions and feelings towards others and yourself. Metta is a type of meditation that is more commonly known as the loving-kindness meditation. Its entire theory rests on developing compassionate thoughts and perceptions toward your inner self. With training, people learn to show gentleness and compassion externally - usually to friends, acquaintances, and lastly, enemies. It is actually proven to be easier to extend compassion and kindness externally than internally. By mastering kindness externally, it helps one give more compassion and kindness to themselves. A recent study consisted of 100 adults; they were assigned at random to a loving-kindness meditation practice program. Researchers found that the benefits of this practice were dependent on dosage. The more effort and time the people put into the loving-kindness meditation, the more positive feelings of kindness they experienced. Another similar study proved that people develop beneficial feelings after practicing loving-kindness meditation can help with anger management, marital conflict, and overall social anxiety. Another conclusion that was drawn in these studies was that these benefits appear to grow over time with the continual practice of this meditation.

Meditation Helps Increase Self-Awareness and Social Skills

Meditation enhances one's self-awareness. Since meditation helps you practice the act of mindfulness, it naturally increases a person's self-awareness. This effect happens because, while practicing mindfulness, you're actually paying attention to your thoughts.

Self-awareness allows you to develop a stronger understanding of yourself and why you think the things you do, which helps you grow into the best version of yourself. This benefit particularly helps people who face social anxiety problems. Being mindful of your actions, facial expressions, tone of voice, and other forms of body language is a great way to know if you're acting in a socially acceptable manner. Having good self-awareness is beneficial as society treats people who have it better than those who don't. It allows you to understand oneself more and, in return, have the ability to understand other people more. Being self-aware actually creates compassion and sympathy, not only for others - but for yourself as well.

Meditation Improves Your Sleep

Meditation helps improve sleep quality and prevents insomnia. Shockingly, nearly 50% of the population in the world will encounter insomnia in their life at some point.

Meditation and mindfulness help you acknowledge and let thoughts pass through your mind, allowing you to clear it of any lingering thoughts. Being able to acknowledge thoughts and let them go plays a huge part in one's ability to fall asleep. If you have many things on your mind, it tends to lead to the inability to fall asleep. It creates stress and anxiety, which is a good night's sleep's worst enemy.

One study related two meditation and mindfulness courses by assigning participants at random to one of two groups. The first group participated in meditation, while the second group did not. The first group who meditated was able to fall asleep quicker and remained asleep longer in comparison to the second group who did not meditate. Becoming experienced in meditation and mindfulness helps one control and redirect the "runaway" or "leftover" thoughts in one's head, which often leads to insomnia. In addition, meditation helps you relax your body, which releases tension. It can then place you into a peaceful state of mind where you will be more likely to fall asleep.

Meditation Helps You Manage Pain.

Meditation can help control pain. Did you know that the origin of the pain is in the brain? This fact is not commonly known. Your perception and feelings of pain are directly connected to your mind and can be emphasized when under stressful conditions.

A study that focused on the relationship or pain and mindfulness used an MRI to watch your brain's activity while participants felt a painful stimulus. Two groups participated in this study. The first group had gone through four days of meditation training, while the second group was not provided any training. The patients who went through the meditation training showed that your brain's area, which controls pain, was highly stimulated. It was also reported that they had a lower sensitivity to pain. In addition to that, a bigger study looked at the aftermath of regular meditators in over 3000participants. Its results were that the meditators were associated with lower companies of intermittent and chronic pain.

Moreover, in a study of patients with terminal illnesses, they found that meditation/mindfulness helped manage and decrease intense pain near the end of their life. In all of the above scenarios, all participants experienced the exact same pain stimuli. Still, those who meditated were more skilled in their ability to handle the pain and even said that they felt a decreased sensation of pain. Overall, the many studies conducted lead to the conclusion that meditation can help people manage their perception of pain. This technique can be used to aid those who experience chronic pain during medical care or physical therapy.

Meditation Helps You Manage Addictions.

Meditation can help fight addictions. This benefit is one of the lesser-known benefits, as it helps a very niche market.

Meditation is, in layman's terms, mental discipline. As we discussed before, you can think of it as mental weight lifting. The mental discipline that you build through meditation is proven to help you work away from dependencies by training self-control and retaliating triggers of behaviors that are addictive.

Scientific research has evidence that meditation can help those increase their understanding of the reasons behind their addiction and help them learn to redirect their attention, increase their willpower and self-control, and control their impulses and emotions. There was a study that taught 20 alcoholics meditation discovered that the volunteers who received this meditation training got better at managing their cravings and the stress related to it.

This training can also help people manage food cravings. Fourteen other research studies showed that mindfulness meditation helped the participants control binge eating and emotional eating episodes.

Meditation Increases Brain Functioning

Meditation is shown to help improve attention span. Have you ever noticed that you are unable to focus on something for an extended amount of time? A common example would be starting to watch a new television show. You may find yourself drifting off after the first two minutes of a new show and end up doing something out of bad habit like scrolling on your phone with the TV playing in the background. This is all due to having a short attention span.

There is a type of meditation called 'focused-attention' meditation that is specifically used to combat this problem. This type of meditation is like lifting weights in the gym for your attention span. Its goal is to help improve the endurance and strength of your attention span.

One recent study looked into the results of an 8-week program of meditation and mindfulness. It found that practicing this specific type of meditation improved the participants' capability to maintain and reorient their focus. A related study focused on human resource employees showed that those who exercised mindfulness practices regularly were able to stay focused longer on any task. In addition, these employees also were able to remember the details of their assignment, whereas their peers who did not use meditation did not.

Another review concluded that meditation could even aid in reversing bad habits in the brain that play a role in worrying and daydreaming. Overall, even briefly meditating can benefit someone's attention span. Another study showed that all you needed was four days of practicing meditation to be able to increase your attention span.

Meditation also helps reduce age-related memory loss. Scientifically, people who don't actively use their brains tend to have them deteriorate faster. This is why in a lot of senior homes, nurses and workers promote brain games for the seniors to prevent deterioration. Games like chess, mahjong, and even video games help exercise your brain's functions to keep it healthy.

Kirtan Kriya is a type of meditation that uses a chant while moving your fingers and hands to help direct your thoughts. It is said to help improve the meditator's ability in memorization tasks in numerous studies that relate to memory loss due to age. A further review of 12 studies discovered that several other meditation practices helped increase memory, attention span, and mental speediness within senior participants. Overall, not only can meditation fight age-related memory loss, it can actually help improve the patient's memory if they are battling dementia. It can also aid those caring for family members with dementia as it is extremely mentally and emotionally taxing.

More Benefits of Mindfulness

This may sound cheesy, but mindfulness really can nourish your soul and open your heart. It helps you gain attributes that you never thought you'd be able to achieve. Things like emotional intelligence, non-judgment, the ability to let go, and self-love. Most people know that these are extremely important to a happy life, but they find it hard to achieve them. There are even more benefits to meditation than those discussed in the previous section. Here we will look at the intangible benefits of meditation.

Mindfulness can open your heart and allow you to be a less judgmental person. A lot of the time, when your mind is cluttered, it's easier to jump to conclusions or associate something you don't understand with something you already know. A common example; when you see someone slacking off at work, you immediately jump to conclude that they are a bad worker and lazy. However, if you allow yourself to be mindful, you can think about WHY you came to that conclusion. You hardly know the person, and there are literally a million other reasons why they would be slacking off today. Perhaps they are not feeling well? Or maybe they're going through a hard time at the moment? These are more reasonable conclusions that you would be unable to draw if you are not mindful. Allowing yourself to be a less judgmental person helps open yourself up to new experiences. How many times did you stop yourself from trying something new just because you "already know" that you wouldn't like it? The answer is probably a lot. The benefit of mindfulness is that you can now be aware when you jump to these conclusions and try to set your judgment aside and try something new. You may be surprised to discover other pleasurable things in life that enrich your day today.

Opening your heart and letting go of judgment produces higher-quality friendships. Have you ever had a friend that is constantly judging others? It really makes you think what they're saying about you when you're not in the room. It's tough to be friends with people who are always judging others. Don't be that person. Through meditation, you now have the ability to recognize when a judgmental thought comes to the forefront of your mind. Acknowledge the judgmental thought and ask yourself why you are thinking about it? Allow yourself to just let that thought go. Resist the temptation of gossiping about other people when you're with friends. This will create a safer and more comfortable environment for your friends. In turn, this develops into closer and higher quality friendships.

Being able to let go of judgment will help you become a happier person. When other people are busy labeling every single thing as good or bad, right or wrong, you are okay with just accepting them for what they are. When you're able to no longer judge things, you achieve more happiness because you're not constantly weighed down by deciphering people's complexities.

Chapter 2: Formal Mindfulness Techniques

Now that you understand some of the many benefits that mindfulness and meditation can offer you, we will begin looking at some specific mindfulness techniques.

For beginners, it is recommended to follow a guided meditation to direct you through the entire process. If nobody is guiding you through this meditation, it is easy to drift away and fall asleep. That is not the purpose of meditation. Throughout this chapter, you will learn about different techniques and how to practice them.

Body Scan Meditation

The first type of meditation we will discuss is commonly known as the Body Scan or Progressive relaxation meditation. The body scan practice is a technique that can be performed multiple times a day to help you identify what you are feeling physically and mentally and where you are feeling it as well. Using this technique, you can learn to release the stress carried in your body and mind. Often, when you are stressed, it's very common for it to be held in different areas of your body in the form of tense shoulders, stomach pains, or in many other ways. You likely are not even aware of the stress that you are carrying in your body! When you are really stressed, you may be feeling a lot of physical discomfort but not necessarily connect it with your emotions.

The BSM method effectively relieves stress not only from the mental aspect but also from the physical aspect. Many research points to the conclusion that there are numerous physical and psychological benefits to relieving tension and relaxing your body. Relieving physical tension has been proven to decrease psychological stress even when you don't use any external stress relief efforts. Relieving tension in your body can likely lead to overall lower levels of stress, which then, as a result, leads to less physical tension. This meditation works to break the vicious cycle of mental and physical tension that can feed on itself. Thus, the body scan meditation is a very effective and useful meditation technique that can help you stay physically and mentally relaxed. It can help you return to a calm state when you notice that you've become too tense. Here is how you can begin practicing BSM:

1. Find a comfortable place where you can sit down and fully relax your body. It's easier if you are lying down but sitting down is effective as well. Try to find a place and

position that is comfortable for you to fully relax but not so comfortable that you may fall asleep easily. Bring your awareness to your breath. Let it slow down and start breathing from deep within your belly instead of your chest. Let your abdomen expand, and then contract with each breath taken. If you find your shoulders moving up and down with each breath, bring your attention to your belly and allow the breathing from there. Pretend as if it's a balloon inflating and deflating your abdomen, everyone you take a breath.

2. This is where we begin to do the actual 'body scan.' Pretend there is a scanner above you (if you are lying down) or in front of you (if you are sitting). Imagine that it expels a horizontal laser beam and slowly scans your body from the top of your head down. Bring your awareness to where that scanner is and slowly move it down your body. Do you notice any tension that you feel as you move the scanner through your body? Do you feel any tightness on your shoulders, neck, back, or stomach? Do you feel any sensations of pain, whether it's subtle or sharp? Are you feeling any areas of concentrated energy in your body? If you notice and feel something that is off, try to acknowledge it and think about why it might be. If there is tension, acknowledge it and move on. Continue to scan your body all the way down, from your scalp to your ears, to your cheeks, to your chin, to your neck, to your shoulders, and so forth. This becomes more automatic and much easier with practice to the point that you will do this very quickly and with less effort.

3. Make sure you're bringing attention to areas that you've discovered to have uncomfortable sensations. Breathe into these areas.

4. Focus on inhaling and exhaling your breath. A lot of people notice that the feelings of tension become more intense at first, so if this happens, do not be alarmed. Continue to meditate through it and simply acknowledge it. Keep your awareness focused on that feeling for a few moments, make sure you are staying present. Move on to the next body part when you're ready.

5. Continue to do this scan with each area of your body, moving from your head to your toes. Make a note of how you feel and which body parts are holding stress. Noticing tension in your body will allow you to be more aware of it in the future.

Try to practice the body scan meditation several times throughout the day or during times where you feel stressed. If you are short on time, you can do an abbreviated version of this meditation by sitting down and bringing awareness to any place in your body where you feel that you are carrying tension.

Breath Awareness Meditation

The second type of meditation we will be discussing is breath awareness meditation. BAM helps combat anxieties and stress that can be caused by our bodies not breathing popularly. Have you ever noticed that you haven't breathed in a while when you are in a stressful situation? BAM can prove very useful in these situations because it helps you train your brain to maintain focus and be mindful, even in the most stressful situations. It's an anchor to revert when your mind wanders off and is pulled away by thoughts, allowing you to remain present.

This type of meditation is also heavily used in yoga culture and yogic customs. This kind of meditation comes into play at each step of the yoga practice. In fact, this is so important that instructors claim that yoga is not yoga without breath awareness. The practice of breath awareness did come from the Buddhists and early Christian teachers as well. This section will learn the technique of breath awareness in meditation and how it's also used in yoga.

Using Breath Awareness during Meditation:

1. Start in a seated position, in a comfortable place with your back straight on a chair, bench, or even a cushion. Close your eyes and rest your body for a few moments. Try to soften the sides of your rib cage along with your abs. Ensuring this posture allows your breath to reach deeper. You will begin to notice a cleansing sensation when you exhale and a feeling of nourishment when you inhale. Be patient and let your breathing guide you. Let your inhale and exhale flow as smoothly as possible. This may take you some time, but eventually, it will feel effortless. When you have achieved this, you are ready to continue to the next step.

2. Next, relax your body, beginning from your head all the way down to your toes. Feel the sensation of relaxation all the way down your body, starting in your feet and ending in your head. Start to slowly move your awareness through the body, and notice where you are tense, just like you do in the body scan technique.

3. When you are finished, return your awareness to your complete body. Breathe with your full body, and imagine every part of you taking a breath. Let yourself follow the effortlessness of your breath. As time goes by, keep paying attention to your breath.

4. Now, notice the feeling of the air flowing into your nostrils. Begin breathing in with your nostrils. Allow it to feel natural and comfortable, and give yourself a some time to do this. Return your awareness to your breathing if your mind starts to wander off. Throughout your practice, remind yourself to focus on your breath anytime you drift off, and try not to break your awareness or breathing. Your mind won't stop thinking, so don't expect it to. Instead, just maintain breath awareness.

5. When thoughts come into your head, let them drift in and out. Do not give them your attention, but do not judge yourself for them either. Just let them go by you like a cloud. As you continue through this exercise, your awareness of your breath will increase. It will slowly

relax you, and you may begin to notice your breath awareness coming about with much more ease. These subtle changes are critical checkpoints for examining your concentration. They act as signals that your breath awareness meditation is working!

Using BAM in Yoga:

1. There are two reclining postures in yoga that we use when people are new to the practice of breath awareness.

   The first is called *Savasana*, which is also known as the corpse pose. This posture is a supine pose, meaning that you are reclining on your back.

   The second is called *Makarasana*. This is also known as the crocodile pose. This pose is achieved by lying on your stomach, face down.

   Savasana is used to achieve and notice abdominal breathing, while the crocodile pose is used to observe the deep, diaphragmatic breathing.

2. Notice your breathing, not only during yoga or meditation but always. Notice it after you climb a long flight of stairs or while you're swimming underwater. The goal here is to be able to watch your own breath without giving it your full attention. We say that in yoga BAM, you try to be a student of your breath.

3. Try to make sure that your yoga breathing is optimal. This requires your breathing to be;
   - Deep
   - Diaphragmatic
   - Nasal
   - Even
   - Smooth
   - Without sound
   - Without pause

4. Once you master your breathing skills in supine and crocodile pose, you will begin to implement these skills in standing postures as well.

Zen Meditation

Zen meditation is a practice that comes from the times of ancient Buddha. This practice comes from the Tang Dynasty of ancient China. The origins of this practice are from China. Still, this popular type of meditation now thrives in Korea, Japan, and many other Asian countries.

The term "Zen" is a Japanese word that derives from the word *Ch'an* in Chinese.

It is also a transformation of *dhyana,* an Indian word meaning meditation or concentration.

Zen meditation is a very old Buddhist meditation discipline, but both beginners and seasoned meditators practice it. One primary benefit of this meditation is the way that it allows a person to examine the inner workings of their mind. This method also provides tools for people to who are dealing with anxiety or depression. However, the main purpose of Zen meditation is rooted in spirituality. It is meant to uncover the clarity of the mind that each of us is capable of achieving.

Different from the basic forms of meditation, Zen meditation encourages a person to look deep within themselves to ponder life's deepest questions. Zen meditation delves deeper than other meditation techniques that focus on relieving stress and relaxing. It is described as "A special transmission outside the teachings; not established upon words and letters; directly pointing to the human heart-mind; seeing nature and becoming a Buddha" by the famous Buddhist master Bodhidharma.

Zen meditation is often learned and practiced in "Schools of Zen." They normally practice this meditation in a seated posture, in the form of something called *zazen*. It begins with sitting upright and following the breath, emphasizing the movement within the belly.

Traditionally, this technique requires a deep and supportive connection from the teacher to their pupil. In this case, it would be a Zen Master and a student of Zen Meditation.

Zen meditation aims to address core issues rather than creating or offering temporary solutions to day-to-day life problems. It explores the true causes of unhappiness and dissatisfaction and redirects our focus in order to bring true understanding. In this theory, the key to joy and wellbeing isn't wealth or fame. In fact, the key lies within all of us. Like other types of spirituality, Buddhism clarifies that the more you give, the more you gain.. According to Zen Buddhism if you look for inner peace, you won't find it. Yet, giving up the idea of a reward and focusing on other people's happiness will create the possibility for lasting peace.

Although you need to train with a Zen master to understand the complicated depths of this spirituality, I will still discuss a few Zen meditation techniques with you. The first is something we recently learned about, which is the observation of the breath.

The second technique is quiet awareness. Here, the meditator will learn to let their thoughts to stream through their minds without rejecting, judging, or grasping. This is similar to the example of watching your thoughts as clouds just pass by you. There is no particular goal to this technique but to just allow their mind to be.

The third technique that Zen meditators use is intensive group meditation. Serious and experienced meditators practice regularly in temples or meditation centers. During this period, the meditators dedicate most of their day to sitting meditation with sessions lasting 30 - 60 minutes. Meals are part of the practice and eaten in silence.

Loving Kindness Meditation

The next meditation technique is called Loving Kindness Meditation (LKM). LKM is a well-liked meditation method that improves self-care, which is used to boost wellbeing and reduces anxiety. People who regularly practice the LKM meditation have an increased capability for internal and external forgiveness, relationships, and the ability to accept themselves. This technique is not difficult and can provide you a sense of calmness.

During the LKM, you focus your loving energy towards others and yourself. In a recently published study in the Harvard Review of Psychology the authors concluded that LKM is beneficial in treating chronic pain and personality disorders. Other published studies have noted that the LKM technique helps manage social anxiety, marriage conflict, and anger. It also suggests that LKM meditation can increase the activation of areas in the brain involved with processing emotions and empathy. This reduces negativity and helps boost a sense of positivity. There are many types of methods to practice LKM, reached based on a different Buddhist tradition. However, each variation is based on the same core psychological operation. During this meditation, you try to generate kind intentions towards internal and external people. Here is a guide on how to practice Loving Kindness Meditation.

1. Set aside a few minutes of quiet time for yourself and sit in a comfortable position. Shut your eyes and begin to relax your muscles. Inhale and exhale a few times deeply.

2. Visualize yourself experiencing physical and psychological wellness along with having inner peace. Try to imagine the feeling of whole and complete love for yourself and thanking your body and yourself for everything that you are and have done. Understanding that you are perfect the way you are. Focus your thoughts onto the feeling of inner peace and imagine yourself exhaling tension and inhaling the feeling of love.

3. Start repeating three to four phrases of positivity to yourself. Try to create your own that is unique to you. Here are a few examples you can also use:
    - "May I be healthy, peaceful, and strong."
    - "May I be happy."
    - "May I be safe."
    - "May I give and receive appreciation today."

4. Let yourself enjoy the feelings of self-compassion for a couple of moments. If you find yourself drifting, gentle redirect your awareness back to these feelings of l kindness and love. Allow these feelings take control of your body and mind.

5. At this point, you can choose either to remain with this focus for the remainder of your meditation or shift to focus on your loved ones in your life. Start with someone with who you are very close, such as your spouse, child, parent, or best friend. Allow yourself to feel your love and appreciation for them. Stay with that feeling. Begin to repeat the phrases we discussed in step three, or create your own that is unique to the person you're focusing on.

6. Once you are able to hold on to these feelings towards that person, start incorporating other people of importance from your life into your awareness. Imagine them with perfect wellness and inner peace, one by one. Then, begin to branch out to other loved ones; friends, family members, neighbors, and even acquaintances. You can even include groups of people from all over the world. Expand the feelings of loving and kindness to humans on the other side of the earth and bring your awareness to the feeling of compassion and human connection. When you are ready, you may even include those with whom you are in a conflict to help reach a place of greater peace and even forgiveness.

7. When you feel like you are ready to end your meditation, open your eyes. Remember that all those wonderful feelings you felt, you can always revisit them throughout the day. Begin to internalize how the LKM meditation feels, and return to those feelings by breathing deeply and shifting your focus.

When you first begin to practice the Loving Kindness Meditation, try to use yourself as the main subject during it. When you begin to get more comfortable with the visualizations and loving phrases, you can begin to add more imagery of others into your meditation. When you have mastered that, you can practice LKM towards the more difficult people in your life. The last and most difficult arm of LKM helps boost feelings of forgiveness, which allows you to let go of negativity within yourself to achieve increased inner peace. The method I have outlined for you is a simple way of getting started with LKM. As you practice it further, you may develop your own LKM technique that works better for you. As long as you can continue to focus your awareness and attention on promoting love and kindness, you can expect to gain benefits from the practice.

Formal Sitting Meditation

The formal sitting meditation can be a combination of different meditation techniques, or you can simply follow your instinct and do what feels good for you.

This particular standardized program focuses on your awareness and bringing your attention to the present. This method has been popularly integrated within medical environments to help treat many health conditions, including stress, pain, and insomnia. Most people do it for at least ten minutes a day, but practicing it for just a couple of minutes each day will lead to positive results in your wellbeing. This is the basic technique that will help you get started:

1. Find a quiet place that you feel comfortable in. Ideally, your home or someone where you feel safe. Sit down on a comfortable chair or any other surface you wish. Make sure you are not tense, and your head and back are straight and aligned.

2. Try to sort your thoughts and then put aside those that are of the past and future. Stick to the thoughts about the present.

3. Bring your awareness to your breath. Make sure to focus on the feeling and sensation of air moving through your body as you inhale and exhale. Feel the way your belly rises and falls. Feel air entering into the nose and exiting through the lips. Make sure to focus on the differences in every inhale & exhale.

4. Observe each thought that comes through your mind. Act as if you are watching the clouds, letting them pass by you as you watch each one. Whether your thought is fear, worry, anxiety, or hope - when these thoughts arise, don't ignore them or suppress them. Simply acknowledge that thought, stay calm, and anchor yourself with your breathing.

5. You may feel as though you are getting absorbed by the thoughts. If this happens, pay attention to where the mind goes, and while avoiding making a judgment, bring your consciousness back to the breath. Keep in mind that this happens a lot with beginners; try not to be too hard

on yourself when this happens. Always use your breathing to bring you back to the present.

6. As we near the end of the 10-minute session, sit for several minutes and bring your awareness to where you are physically right now. Gradually stand up.

Chapter 3: Informal Mindfulness Techniques

Mindfulness is an awareness practice that you use to bring your mind away from thoughts that are not of the present moment. In this chapter, we will look at some of the less formal mindfulness techniques that can be used in your everyday life when you are short on time or when you cannot get yourself to an appropriate location for formal meditation practice.

Mindfulness Meditation

The most original and standardized program for mindfulness meditation is called the Mindfulness-Based Stress Reduction (MSBR) program. I will be teaching you how to conduct this meditation in your own home. This meditation was developed by a Ph.D. student who was a student of a famous Buddhist monk. This program focuses on helping the individual bring their awareness to the present and to focus on their own awareness. This meditation has increased in popularity and is not incorporated into medical settings to treat health conditions such as anxiety, insomnia, pain, and stress. Although this meditation is quite straightforward, professionals recommend you find a teacher or a program that can act as a guide when you begin. The ideal amount of time you should be spending on mindfulness meditation is at least 10 minutes per day.

Mindfulness Meditation Transcript

Here is the step by step instructions on how you can do this meditation:

1. Find a place that is quiet and you feel comfortable in. Ideally, this is your home or a place where you feel safe. Sit in something comfortable like a chair and make sure your head and back are straight and aligned. Try to release any tension you feel.

2. Begin to sort your thoughts and put away the ones that are of the past or future. Focus on your thoughts that are about the present.

3. Begin to bring your awareness to your breath. Focus on the sensation of air moving through your body when you inhale and exhale. Focus on this feeling. Begin to feel the movement of your belly as it rises and falls. Feel how the air enters through your nostrils and leaves through your mouth. Pay attention to how each breath is different.

4. Watch your thoughts come and go in front of you. Pretend you are watching the clouds, letting them slowly pass before you. It doesn't matter if your thought is a worry, anxiety, hope, or fear - when these thoughts pass by, don't ignore them or suppress them. Simply just acknowledge them calmly and anchor yourself by focusing on your breathing.

5. If you find yourself being carried away by your thoughts, observe where your mind drifted off to and without judging yourself, simply anchor yourself by focusing on your breathing. This happens a lot with beginners, so don't be hard on yourself if you drift away. Always use your breathing as an anchor.

6. When you are nearing the end of your 10-minute session, sit still for two minutes and bring awareness to your physical location. Get up slowly.

Everyday Breathing and Observing Technique

Breath awareness exercises are there to help you calm down when you are feeling strong negative feelings such as anxiety and stress. Using breath awareness exercises will help you combat anxieties and stress that can be caused by our bodies not breathing popularly. Have you ever noticed that you haven't breathed in a while when you are in a stressful situation? We will learn more about how to combat unhealthy breathing habits that can lead to a decline in physical and psychological health.

Achieving mindful observation is incredibly powerful because it helps you become more aware and appreciate your environment's simple elements in a more profound way. There are a lot of beautiful aspects in our life that we tend to overlook just because our mind is used to them. By achieving mindful observation, you can find simple joys in life, such as; a sunny day, the smell of freshly cut grass, or the soft fur of your cat. Over time, many people who haven't achieved mindful observation tend to resent the place where they reside. For example, they may only begin to notice the bad parts of the apartment they are living in instead of noticing the good. In human nature, it is easy for what is good to become your norm, which takes away from its beauty.

Everyday Breathing Exercise

Let's try a mindful observation exercise.

1. Choose a natural object within your current environment and focus on just watching it for a couple of minutes. This could be a plant or an insect, or even the clouds or the moon.

2. Don't do anything else except notice the object you are watching. Simply relax and watch it for long as your concentration will let you.

3. Look at this object as if you are seeing it for the first time.

4. Explore this object visually by focusing on its formation, and allow yourself to be consumed by its presence.

5. Allow yourself to connect with its energy and its natural purpose in the world.

Improving your mindful observation is important to help us better cope with difficult thoughts and feelings that cause us stress and anxiety. By cultivating the moment-by-moment awareness in our surroundings, we achieve mindful observation. If we regularly practice mindfulness meditations, we will harness the ability to anchor the mind in the present moment instead of being influenced by negative experiences of the past and fears of the future. When we master this, we will be able to deal with life's challenges in a clear-minded and calm way.

Spiritual Mindfulness Technique

This meditation is used for those who want to explore spirituality further. You may not feel any different during this meditation, but you will feel the physical and mental benefits of this practice. During this meditation, you will have to be awake. This technique can lead to sleep. Avoid that to experience spiritual effects.

Before we begin this meditation, think about your own spirituality. What gives you meaning in life? You will need to come up with a word or a short phrase that gives you meaning. You will repeat those words during the time it takes to exhale a breath. For example, if nature holds deep and strong meaning for you, you may select phrases that relate to it.

"Welcome to the Spiritual Meditation.

Find a comfortable position for you, one that allows you to remain awake.

Let's begin.

Close your eyes. You can choose to focus your gaze on a small area. Start by relaxing your muscles and relieving any tension you feel.

When you feel thoughts come to your mind, simply acknowledge them and let them pass. Bring your attention back to your body.

Bring your awareness to your breathing. Notice the way each breath feels. Don't try to change your breathing; let it be natural. Just observe.

As thoughts arise in your mind, acknowledge them and let them go. Return your attention to breathing.

Breathe slowly, deeply, and naturally.

If you find your thoughts wandering some more, bring your attention to breathing.

Notice how your breath flows gently in and out through your body. It feels effortless.

Interruptions are normal. You may find yourself thinking about other thoughts. Let them go, and focus on breathing.

Now, begin to think about the meaningful words or phrases you've selected. Begin to say this word in your mind as you breathe out.

Each time you exhale, say the phrase again.

Continue repeating the phrase every time you breathe out.

With each breath, allow distracting thoughts to float by your awareness.

Let any spiritual feeling linger in your body. Don't ignore it, but let it brew deeply inside you. Let it consume your body and let it stay.

Repeat the phrase. Feel the spirituality within you intensify. You may leave this meditation at any moment; simply open your eyes.

Let your body communicate and get comfortable with the feeling of spirituality. Be aware of how it makes you feel.

Begin to bring your awareness back to your breath. Breathe in. Breathe out. Let your thoughts turn to your body. Relaxed, peaceful, and calm. Notice how your body feels as it becomes more aware of your surroundings.

Bring your attention back to your thoughts. Bring it back to your regular conscious awareness. You may let the spirituality leave your body.

Stay seated for a few more moments with your eyes open. Enjoy the feeling of reawakening. Savor the relaxation and all the other feelings you've encountered.

Begin to reflect on the experience of spiritual meditation. Be aware of all the feelings during the practice. You should be feeling free from worries.

End this guided meditation by wiggling your toes and then your fingers. Stretch your back and shoulders. When you are ready, you may stand up and continue on with your day."

Happy Mind Meditation

This meditation can be used for a time of stress and anxiety. It will help guide you into a more relaxed state where you can focus on the present and find inner peace. Please use this meditation method when you find your mind racing. You can also use this if you feel like you are about to have an anxiety or panic attack.

"Welcome to the happy mind guided meditation.

Please find yourself in a quiet area to sit and dim the lighting.

Make sure you are comfortable. Sit with your back straight and shoulders relaxed. Loosen any tight clothing that may be restricting you.

Let your hands lie loosely and relaxed into your lap. Close your eyes and take a deep breath. Now, relax.

Now that your eyes are closed, you may begin to connect with your inner self of thoughts and feelings.

Gradually, let the outside world fade from your awareness.

For the next few minutes, allow yourself to enjoy and submerge into this relaxing experience.

You are free from all your responsibilities during this meditation. Any thoughts, tasks, or concerns that you may have do not require your immediate attention. Tuck those thoughts away and focus on your inner thoughts.

You may find that your mind will begin to wander during this meditation. This is okay, and this is normal. Simply bring your awareness back to the present and to the sound of my voice. I will guide you into a place of inner peace and deep relaxation.

Remember that you are always in control of yourself. If you wish to end this meditation, you can do so by opening your eyes.

Begin to take a slow, long, and deep breath in through your nose. Release that breath through your mouth.

Find your inner self begin to relax.

Begin to take another deep breath in and exhale.
Notice how it is calming this type of breathing is. Be aware of the feelings of relaxation starting to spread throughout your body, starting from your lungs all the way down to your toes.

Continue to breathe deeply, slowly, and gently. Try not to breathe too quickly.

With each inhales and exhale, your thoughts start to become lighter.

You may start to feel a sense of spaciousness inside of you. It will open up slowly.

Keep relaxing.

Allow the soft movement of your breath to guide you into an even more relaxed state of being.

Breathe in. Breathe out. Deeper you go into this state of relaxation.

Breathe in. Breathe out. Let your mind gradually slow down. Breathe in. Breathe out. Let it slow down some more.

Breathe in. Breathe out.

You are now in a state of relaxation. You may now begin to enjoy a guided journey into your inner place of joy and serenity.

Allow images and visualizations to form in your mind naturally, as I speak. Do so at your own pace.

If visualizations and mental pictures aren't coming easily to you, sense your imaginary surroundings instead of visualizing them.

Begin to let your expectations drift away from you. Let them go. Allow yourself to experience this meditation journey in whatever form comes naturally to you.

Begin to imagine that you are standing in a green and beautiful grassy field. The field stretches on for miles. You can feel the heat of the sun on your face, slowly warming your body.

You feel the soft and lush green grass cushioning your bare feet. You can smell nature all around you.

You can hear the sounds of nature around you. You hear the rustling of the blowing grass. Birds are singing—the rustling of leaves in the distance.

You feel very much at home in this serene place.

You have all the time in the world.

You are safe and happy here.

Take a moment to appreciate your surroundings.

You notice a large luscious tree growing close by.

You begin to walk towards that tree.

Take your time walking. There is no rush whatsoever. Stay in the moment and appreciate the feeling of each step.

As you walk towards the tree, you feel yourself falling more deeply into a state of relaxation.

You are now standing under the tree. Its long branches and large leaves hang right above your head.

You notice that the tree holds many delicious fruits in all shapes, sizes, and colors.

This is not just an ordinary tree. Its fruits carry special powers.

Reach your arm up and take a piece of fruit from the branches. Watch it for a moment. Notice the color of this fruit, the texture, and the weight. It's quite heavy in your hand.

Take a bite of this fruit.

As you swallow the fruit, it slides down your throat and into your belly. You begin to feel something wonderful happen.

A feeling of happiness and peace begins to glow inside of your body.

The sensation starts in your abdomen, and it spreads to your chest and into your heart.

Let go of thinking, and begin to bring all your attention to the feeling. Embellish in the sensation of joy, love, and peace. Feel your body gently glowing with these feelings.

Take another bite of the magical fruit. Taste it. Savor every bite.

This wonderful feeling begins to intensify even more.

Feel yourself begin to radiate this beautiful sensation of love and happiness.

Take another bite of the fruit. Take as many bites as you'd like.

Relax and let yourself drown in this enchanting feeling. Instead of trying, just let it effortlessly take over. Break down any walls that you feel comfortable breaking and let them surround you as much as you like.

Stay with these joyful and peaceful feelings. Enjoy this time of meditation.

You may remain in this relaxed state of meditation for as long as you please. Don't feel rushed to leave."

When you are ready, you may finish this meditation. Simple open your eyes to leave. Take a deep breath and give yourself a few moments to adjust before standing up.

Gratitude Meditation

The Gratitude Meditation is used as a conscious effort to appreciate all the things in the world that makes us feel good. It is directly related to opening our hearts and embracing all our blessings. This meditation is very popular amongst Buddhist monks and nuns. It's typically practiced at the beginning and end of their days to pay gratitude to everything that helped them throughout that day; this also includes their sufferings. Gratitude meditation gives us the power we need to face our problems and weaknesses to acknowledge the darker parts of life. This meditation can be used when you are feeling the burdens of the world. Try this guided meditation when you feel self-pity or hopeless.

Before you begin this meditation, think about something in your life that you are grateful for. Think about where that feeling is held in your body. You can feel grateful for your home, spouse, or even the vacation you just purchased.

"Welcome to the Gratitude Meditation.

Find a comfortable sitting position and dim the lighting.

I will begin by bringing your awareness to the things you are grateful for in life.

Give the sense of gratitude the chance to come up naturally. When it arises, let yourself sink into that feeling. Surrender yourself to it. Begin to notice how it feels inside your body, how that energy feels. If the feeling of gratitude does not come up immediately, don't try to force yourself. It is okay. Instead, just surrender yourself to your heart and not your head.

Let's begin to travel through the aspects of your life that you are thankful for. Bring your awareness back to your breath. As you breathe in and breathe out, begin to think about how each breath gives you life.

Bring your awareness to your heart now. Feel it beating, pulsing, filling your body with everything it needs. Feel it being filled with love, joy, and compassion. Feel the peace. Let all these feelings flow through you with each pump.

Now bring your awareness to your ears. Hear the joyous sounds of music, laughter, silence, and the voices of the people you love. Take in the beautiful sounds of life.

Bring your awareness to your face and then to your nose. Remember the smells of the ocean, freshly cut grass, the aroma of freshly baked bread, flowers, nature, the smells that come from the kitchen, and pastries in the oven.

Slowly bring your awareness to your lips. Allow it to travel into your mouth. Remember the delicious tastes of food and drinks. The feeling of kisses and laughter. Thank your lips for all the laughter and singing it has produced.

Direct your awareness to your hands. Thank it for everything it has done for you. Allow yourself to feel the feelings of touch, caress, applaud, and squeezing. These are the arms and shoulders that you have used to hug and hold.

Bring your awareness now down to your feet. Wiggle your toes. Your feet have served you well. They transported you, allowed you to walk, run, dance, kick, and leap. Be thankful for them.

Now bring your awareness to your inner self. Your sorrows, tears, and strength that you muster every day to make it through. Thank your inner self for always being there.

Direct your awareness to your growth. Be aware of how you have grown and how your perspective has changed. Be grateful for your ability to see growth and potential in life and other people. Acknowledge your empathy and understanding.

Now, just focus on breathing. Breathe in. Breathe out. Let it be graceful.

Start to experience the warmth, compassion, love, and peace that gratitude brings into your body and into your heart. Savor that feeling. Remember it. Remember that it is always there inside of you. You just have to summon it.

Direct your awareness to the relationships in your life. They have nurtured you at some point in your life. Acknowledge the new ones and the old ones.

Thank all the material things that you have had in your life. Whether they came expectedly or unexpectedly, be grateful for the things you have achieved with commitment and hard work.

Begin to think of love in your life. Think about how the connection feels to those things that are just right.

Remind yourself that when we don't take life for granted, we become thankful for everything that we have.

Breathe in. Breathe out. Let that feeling flow through your body again.

When you are ready to end this meditation, simply just open your eyes.

Stretch your back and shoulders. Take one last deep breath, and carry on about your day."

Chapter 4: Mindfulness in Everyday Life

Mindfulness meditation is the simplest type of meditation, as we learned in the previous chapter; however, you can still practice mindfulness without having to meditate. There are a few opportunities in your day where you can practice mindfulness. In this chapter, I will provide you with several suggestions for where you can easily find the time to practice mindfulness.

Physical Mindfulness

Becoming mindful of your physical body is just as important as being mindful mentally. We do many activities daily using our bodies that we don't think about, which causes us to lose mindfulness. Have you ever felt yourself go into autopilot while driving to work? Or going into autopilot when you're waiting in a line? These are common things that the human body naturally does to help us save energy throughout the day. To improve our mindfulness, we must overcome our natural tendencies to go into autopilot when doing tasks that our body is habitually used to. This chapter will learn about how to be mindful with your observation, commuting, and working. These are three aspects that everyone experiences constantly in their life. I will also teach you about being mindful of your own physical health by paying attention to the activities and foods you are giving to your body. Learning to be more mindful of your own health will not only help you live a healthier life it will also teach you to be more mindful and add value to your goal of mindfulness.

As I mentioned earlier, being mindful of your physical health is just as important as practicing meditation. If you cannot pay attention to what you are putting your body through, you are actually affecting your overall mindfulness. People who regularly participate in unhealthy activities like drinking alcohol, smoking, and infrequent exercising are actually fueling their autopilot function to serve instant gratification. Learning to pay attention to your physical health will help you realize that certain unhealthy activities you're used to making you 'feel good' don't actually make you feel good. We know that practicing mindfulness helps people decrease feelings of stress, anxiety, and depression. Here are some other areas that bring mindful of your physical health can help with:

- **Stress reduction:** When a person is suffering from a lot of stress, it intensifies their depression or anxiety and increases their risk of developing more serious depression or anxiety disorders. Try to make changes in your life that can help you reduce or manage stress. Identify which aspects of your life creates the most stress, such as unhealthy relationships or work overload, and find ways to minimize their impact and the stress it brings.

- **Exercise:** Researchers have found that regularly exercising can be just as effective as medication when it comes to treating depression and anxiety. Exercises boost the 'feel-good' brain chemicals in the brain, such as serotonin and endorphins. These chemicals also trigger the growth of new brain cells and connections similar to what antidepressants do. The best part about exercise is that you don't need to do it intensely in order to have the benefits. Even a simple 30-minute walk can make a huge difference in a person's brain activity. For the best results, people should aim to do 30 – 60 minutes of aerobic activity every day or on most days.

- **Nutrition:** The ability to eating properly is imperative for everyone's mental and physical health. By eating smalls meals that are well-balanced throughout the day, you can minimize your mood swings and keep your energy levels up. Although you may crave sugary foods due to the quick boost of energy that it can bring, complex carbohydrates are much more nutritious. Instead, complex carbohydrates can provide you with an energy boost without a crash at the end.

- **Social Support:** Having a strong social network reduces isolation, which is a huge risk factor in depression and anxiety. Make an effort to keep in regular contact with family and friends (ideally on a daily basis) and consider joining a support group or class. You can also opt to do some volunteering where you can get the social support you need while helping others as well.

- **Sleep:** A person's sleep cycle has strong effects on mood. When a person does not get enough sleep, their symptoms of depression or anxiety may get worse. Sleep deprivation causes other negative symptoms like sadness, fatigue, moodiness, and irritability. Not many people can function well with less than seven hours of sleep per night. A healthy adult should be aiming for 7 – 9 hours of sleep every night.

Mindful Eating

The lack of mindful eating is something most of our population suffers from due to our lives' increased pace. We typically find ourselves eating at work in front of our computer, or eating dinner in front of the TV, or even eating during the commute to work! This seemingly small problem is actually one of the leading factors in today's obesity and eating disorder problem. To combat this, we need to improve our ability to eat mindfully. Mindful eating uses the act of mindfulness to help overcome common eating problems in our fast-paced lives. The goal here is to shift focus from external thinking while eating to exploring and enjoying the eating experience itself. This is done in order to develop a new mindset around food. Here are a couple of points to help yourself identify when you are eating mindlessly.

- You are consistently eating until you are overly full or even feel sick.
- You find yourself nibbling on food without really tasting it.
- You aren't paying any attention to the foods you are eating and frequently eat in places that surround you with distractions.
- You are rushing through your meals.

- You have trouble remembering what you ate, or even the taste and smell of the last meal you've consumed.

How To Eat Mindfully

If you find yourself relating to the points above, you may want to actively practice mindful eating. Practicing mindful eating will enhance your enjoyment of meals, prevent overeating, help with digestion, reduce anxiety surrounding food, and improve your psychological relationship with food. Follow these quick exercises below to increase your mindfulness while eating.

- **Exercise #1: Prioritize your mealtimes.**

Try to isolate a 15-minute block to sit down and enjoy your meal. Don't eat on the go or skip meals because you're 'too busy.' Make sure you are always making time to eat at least three meals per day, no matter how busy you are.

- **Exercise #2: Avoid distractions while you are eating**

It is impossible to enjoy eating your food when your attention is somewhere else. Try asking yourself how often you eat while in front of the TV, in the car, or in front of the computer? Under those circumstances, eating is always mindless and can lead to overeating, choosing unhealthy options, or not enjoying your meal at all.

- **Exercise #3: Avoid being rushed around during meal times**

Schedule a time block to eat your meal when you don't have any distractions around you. Even eating with a coworker or a friend may be a distraction due to conversation.

- **Exercise #4: Always sit down to eat your meal**

Try and avoid eating while standing up or walking as these create distractions. When you are physically up and about while eating, it will cause your mind to become distracted at the task at hand as you will have to concentrate on your movement.

- **Exercise #5: Serve your meal on a plate or bowl**

If possible, serve it on your favorite plate or bowl. Avoid eating food from the packet or take out containers as it makes eating feel less formal. This will help you pay more attention to your meal and its physical appearance.

- **Exercise #6: Make a conscious effort to chew your food thoroughly**

Many people find themselves swallowing too soon and end up with digestion problems. Give your stomach an easier time digesting by breaking down the food properly before swallowing.

- **Exercise #7: Make sure to eat only until you're 80% full**

This is a fine line. Don't eat until you are certain you are full, but eat until you feel satisfied. A lot of the time, the feeling of fullness comes 10 minutes after you finish your meal. If you find yourself feeling full while you are still eating, you probably have overeaten.

- **Exercise #8: Take your time to truly savor the taste of food**

Use all five of your senses. Before eating, take a look at your meal of its look, smell, and overall appeal. Think about how each ingredient was cooked and seasoned and how you think the dish would taste because of it. During the meal, identify the taste of all the ingredients. What is the flavor? How does the flavor change if I eat different combinations of the ingredients? What can you smell? How does the texture feel in your mouth?

- **Exercise #9: Ask yourself how you feel about the food you are consuming**

Do you feel happy? Pleasure? Guilt? Regret? Stress? Disappointment? Pay attention to the thoughts that the food brings to your mind. Does it bring up any memories? Fears? Beliefs? How does your body feel after the meal compared to before? Do you feel energetic after the meal, or do you feel lethargic? Does your stomach feel full or empty?

- **Exercise #10: Try to prepare your own meals where it is possible**

The act of preparing food is proven to be psychologically beneficial and therapeutic. Make sure you are touching, tasting, and smelling the individual ingredients.

- **Exercise #11: Make a note of the difference in good food**

This tends to be food that is fresh, seasonal, and minimally processed. Fresh and organic food tends to improve your overall mood and health. Food is our body's nourishment, and it provides the nutrition necessary for us to function optimally. Ingesting better quality food and ingredients is crucial to helping you feel better physically and psychologically.

Practicing meditation is your first step in being able to achieve mindful eating. Allowing yourself to be mindful in your day to day life will bring new joys and satisfactions that have always been there but have not been noticed in some time.

Mindful Commuting

This is one of those activities where it's easy for people to do mindlessly. This is especially relevant if you are driving the same route every day. Make use of this time by not letting your mind wander off to think about tasks that you need to do that day. Practice mindfulness by trying to keep yourself anchored. Take in sensations and visuals like the color of the car in front of you, the smell of your own car, and the feeling of the steering wheel. Focus your attention on all the sounds and noises you hear. If you find yourself wandering, bring your attention back to where you are in your car.

We can all agree that one of the most dreaded daily activity is the commute to work. In fact, according to many studies, this is so dreaded that a long commute is actually one of the major stressors in life that decreases happiness. The easy answer in this situation is to just move and live closer to where you work and keeping your commute short. However, unless you have tons of money - this may not be feasible for many. So, how do we increase our happiness during the awful chore of the commute? The answer is to practice mindful commuting. By practicing meditation, you have achieved an increased level of mindfulness. Take that one step further and extend that mindfulness not only during meditation time but during your commute as well.

Let's use the example of driving to work. This is the perfect place to practice mindfulness. It helps keep the anger and stress at bay when we encounter situations that induce road rage. Rather than finishing your drive stressed out and upset, you can end your drive feeling refreshed and ready to work. It's extremely easy to tune things out and get lost in your thoughts while driving. For some reason, our autopilot takes over, and you get to the office safely (most of the time). Mindful driving is all about being present during the actual drive. It allows us to move away from obsessive and negative thoughts and gives us a chance to appreciate the world we live in.

Mindful Commuting Exercise

Here are some exercises you can do the next time you are commuting:

1. When you first get into your car, take a few controlled breaths. Acknowledge that you are now in your car and are about to start driving.

2. Turn off your radio and keep your phone on silent. Try to eliminate all potential distractions that could occur in your drive.

3. Take a moment to take in your surroundings and the silence in your car. What color is your dashboard? Do you hear the rumbling of your engine?

4. As you begin to drive, start paying attention to your surroundings. You may begin to notice different things on the route to work that you've never noticed before. Take in the sights, sounds, and scenery of your drive.

5. Focus your attention on the physical experience of driving. Pay attention to where your hands are placed on the steering well. What does it feel like sitting in your seat? How do the pedals feel against the sole of your shoe?

6. Begin to shift your focus to other physical sensations in your body. Do you feel the tension in your shoulders or in your neck? Do you have a headache? Do your hips feel tight from sitting for long periods? Relax the parts of your body that feel tense, and you will start to feel some of the pain and stress leave your body.

7. Suppose you encounter a stressful situation while driving, such as being cut off. Try to notice the feelings that this brings. Does it bring your frustration? Anger? Anxiety? Maybe even induce some competitiveness? Acknowledge and identify these emotions and understand why you are feeling them. Often times, simply understanding why you feel a negative emotion will help you feel less negative.

8. When you stop at a red light or stop sign, take a moment and do a quick breathing exercise. Take a few deep and calming breaths 3 - 4 times before you start the car again.

9. Any time your mind begins to wander, gently pull your awareness back to the present. An untrained mind naturally jumps from topic to topic quickly. Statistically, the average person thinks as many as 50,000 different thoughts every day. You can't stop it completely during but practicing mindful driving will redirect these monkeying thoughts to focus on the actual act of driving. Remember, when you notice yourself thinking about anything that is not the task at hand - take a deep breath and bring your awareness back.

Overall, meditation, in general, helps with mindfulness in your day. Being able to take it one step further and focusing on mindful observation, eating, and commuting, will help you decrease stress levels and bring more happiness into your day.

Mindful Bedtime Routine

This is normally the time where you begin to get things ready for the next day. Instead of battling too much with it, just keep in mind what needs to be done. Stop trying to rush through it to get to bed but try to enjoy the experience of completing those actual tasks. Focus on what needs to be done and don't think about what is next. Start early to leave yourself with enough time, so you don't need to rush through things. Any thoughts or anxieties that come up should be acknowledged and let go.

Mindful Exercising

Make your workout routine a time to also exercise mindfulness. Try to exercise without screens or music and focus only on your breathing and where your feet are moving. Although watching TV or listening to music will make your workout go by faster or distract you from any anxiety, it won't help manage any unhealthy thoughts. Bring your attention to feeling how your muscles feel and pay attention to how your body reacts to your workout. Instead of ignoring the pains you may be feeling, acknowledge it and let yourself feel the exercise.

Mindful Teeth Brushing

Since you have to brush your teeth every day, you can use this time frame to practice mindfulness. Start by feeling your weight against the floor, the feeling of your toothbrush in your hand, and the feeling of movement as you begin brushing your teeth. Focus on these feelings and the thoughts you are having in the present. Don't dwell; just acknowledge those thoughts as they come and go.

Mindful Dish Washing

This is a wonderful window of time where you can use to practice mindfulness. Typically, when you are doing the dishes, there isn't anyone trying to get your attention. This is a perfect time to try mindfulness. Try to focus on the feeling of warm water on your hands, the look and feel of bubbles, the smell of your dish soap, and sounds of your plates clunking water. Try to give yourself to this experience and feel your mind refreshing and your anxiety fading.

Mindful Working

We have all had the experience of feeling overwhelmed and scattered at work. This could be caused by too many projects or a sense of demotivation to complete current assignments. Did you know that motivation in the workplace is directly linked to mindfulness? Our ability to stay focused and mindful at work is a way to reprogram our minds to think healthier and less stressful. Below are some benefits to how mindful working can improve your everyday life.

First off, mindfulness in the workplace helps with stress reduction. This is a dominant cause of employee disengagement. The European Agency for Safety and Health at Work conducted a study that produced the statistic that more than half of 550 million working days are lost every year from absenteeism are stress-related. In addition, 80% of employees report that they feel stress from their workplace and need help learning how to manage it. Some forward-thinking companies nowadays, such as Google and Adobe, all have formal mindfulness programs incorporated into the workplace to promote stress reduction in employees. However, if you are already practicing meditation, you don't need to worry if your workplace doesn't offer a program like this. You can do it yourself.

Mindfulness in the workplace also leads to higher absorption of new information. Scientific facts point to allowing your brain to break from developing new skills, critical thinking, and problem-solving to increase learning and creativity. Not taking enough breaks altogether leads to increased tiredness, stress, and thinking blocks. This holds especially true for those who work in jobs that require an extended period of focus.

Adaptability is something that can increase when you are mindful at work. Being able to adapt quickly and efficiently is crucial at work. Did you know that most employers nowadays value resourcefulness and adaptability over hard skills like coding or programming? Adaptability means that you can quickly adjust accordingly to new situations and handle multiple requests at once. The more you expose yourself to different ways of doing tasks, learning, and gaining confidence in moments of uncertainty, the more adaptable you will become. Adaptability is one of the most important characteristics of excellent leadership performance. It's typically present in leaders who are able to manage changing priorities and are comfortable in adjusting their own perceptions and beliefs.

Problem-solving abilities are enhanced when you are mindfully working. Problem-solving is the ability to remove chaos from the untrained mind. Removing that clutter leads to better concentration, which ultimately leads to untying the complicated knot of problem-solving. In addition, mindfulness helps with problem-solving by freeing you from distractions and giving you a new angle to attack from. When you are at the heart of a challenge, try to practice mindfulness. You may be surprised at the increased ability to process information in different ways that are required for a resolution.

Being mindful in the workplace also helps facilitate creativity. The fundamental aspect of creativity is divergent thinking. This refers to the ability to come up with ideas that are outside the box. By practicing mindfulness at work, you may be able to enhance creativity, which allows you to think more innovatively than those who are mindless. Mindfulness helps free your mind from distractions, which in turn boosts your ability to look at things around you from a new perspective.

Vitality in the workplace is also strengthened when you are working in a mindful manner. By definition, vitality means 'exuberant physical strength of mental vigor.' In our case, mindfulness increases a person's vitality, or in other words; their mental vigor. Every single day you go to work with a certain amount of energy. Some days if you've had a healthy sleep, you may have high energy. Some days if you've had a rough night's sleep, you may feel like you're running on an empty gas tank. Vitality is an essential element in accomplishing tasks while being able to enjoy the work you are doing at the same time. Continuing to stay focused and mindful is proven to positively affect your vitality as it helps you remember your goals and dreams. When your aspirations are clear to you, you are more likely to work towards them when you've got high vitality.

When you are working mindfully in the workplace, you'll likely notice that you have increased empathy towards others. We've all heard the saying "to stand in someone else's shoes." Empathy plays a huge role in understanding the minds of other people and relating emotionally with others. Practicing mindfulness at work enables us to have the room in our brain that is used to feel empathy for other people.

Chapter 5: How to Find the Right Kind of Meditation for You

Now that you understand the benefits of mindfulness and have seen numerous examples of how you can practice it, I will teach you how to determine which technique is best for you. In this chapter, we will also look at some of the best habits that you can employ to help you achieve mindfulness in your daily life. Let's dive in!

Each person reading this book has a different reason that brought them here. Each person's reasoning as to why they want to learn how to become mindful will vary slightly, but the root of everyone's reasons are the same; you want to change your life for the better!

If you are unsure of your motive or your "why," take some time to look deep within yourself and address the reasons why you are reading this book or the reasons why you feel it is time to make a change in your life. By taking stock of your feelings, will lead you to find your motivation for seeking change. Whatever your objective, writing it down will help to solidify it and make it more real. By having it written down on paper, you will have put your reason for doing all of this out into the universe, and it will make you feel as if there is no going back now. This will keep you motivated when times get tough. You can revisit that paper anytime you need a reminder of why you are taking on such a challenge. Seeing that paper will remind you of why it is all worth it.

Understanding the specific reasons you want to learn mindfulness and meditation will be the most important part of your journey. This is because having a strong reason *why* will keep you motivated, even when the process is difficult.

Take some time before continuing to find out your reasons for seeking this book in the first place. Are you learning to meditate because you are under a lot of stress? Was meditation recommended by your therapist to help with your anxiety? Do you simply want to do this to find more peace in your day to day life?

How to Find the Right Mindfulness and Meditation Technique

Up until this point, we've discussed numerous health benefits of meditation and the most common issues that it can help treat. You have also learned about numerous different kinds of meditation techniques. Understanding what you need help with will help you pick the right meditation to use in your own life.

Below, we will look at the steps that you should take to determine which type of meditation is best for you. The first step in determining what type of meditation is best for your life is to assess your current needs.

1.   Rank Your Needs

Start with what you want to achieve. This can be anything from lowering anxiety to easing shoulder pains. You can have one goal or multiple; try to rank them from most important to least important.

2.   Assess Your Lifestyle

Next, assess what kind of lifestyle you lead right now. Are you living in a fast-paced city? Or a slow-paced and comfortable countryside? Or maybe you live somewhere in between the two? Assess how much time you'd be able to put into meditation.

For those who have more free time in their days, set aside a specific time of day to practice it every day of the week. For those with less time on their hands, think of moments you will have during your busy day to use for meditation. As discussed earlier, this can be during your commute to work or during the time you're washing your dishes.

3.   Match Your Needs

Next, determine what type of meditation method suits you the best. Out of the six types of meditation we've discussed, four of them are the most accessible to your average human:

mindfulness meditation, Body Scan, Loving and kindness, and breath awareness.

Mindfulness meditation tends to help people with anxiety issues, whereas the body scan tends to help with releasing stress in the body. On the other hand, loving-kindness meditation tends to focus more on the emotional aspects of a person's life, while breath awareness meditation focuses on managing a person's breathing, which is great for stress and anxiety.

Pick one that you resonate with most and that helps with the particular problem you're hoping to solve. The most common form of meditation chosen out of the four is the mindfulness meditation method, as it tends to help with the most ailments and is the easiest for beginners to practice.

4. Assess Your Spirituality

Next, assess your spirituality.

Are you a spiritual person or not? Determining this will help you decide how far and deep you want to take your meditation practices. Of course, this isn't something you need to determine from day one; you can determine that throughout your journey of meditation.

A lot of people who are very spiritual from the get-go tend to jump right into deeper-level courses.

There are many modern retreats nowadays in Asia and South East Asia that you can sign up for, which will teach you the ways of spirituality within meditation and how they relate to one another.

Coming to a decision on which type of meditation practice suits you the best may be easy for some and hard for others. Don't worry; you can do multiple types of meditation throughout the day and pick the ones that suit you the most to incorporate into your day to day life. Remember, meditation does not come naturally to many of us, and it's okay to fall off the train. What is important is not giving up and continuing to make an effort to make it an integral part of your day and life. One of the most difficult parts of meditation is the lack of direction and accountability. Unless you have a Guru at your side who is holding you accountable - it is entirely up to you to keep practicing meditation. Once you get going in your journey, I recommend signing up for meditation or yoga classes regularly to have someone there to hold you accountable. It's amazing what even a few sessions of meditation can do for the mind and body.

Habits to Increase Mindfulness in Everyday Life

Now, let's take a look at a few exercises and habits that will help you improve your physical mindfulness. Begin by incorporating one of these exercises into your daily routine and begin to incorporate more when they have become habits. By slowly incorporating all of these exercises, you will find that you have become more mindful of your physical health and your body's feelings.

- **Exercise #1: Taking daily breaks and time outs**

Making the time to take a couple 'time outs' a day is crucial in letting an individual's mind rest from all the mental exercise. You can do this by scheduling at least one 15-minute block a day where you find somewhere quiet and private to sit by yourself. During this time, you can practice something that can ground you into the present to help you focus on that rather than the whirlwind of thoughts caused by anxiety. For example, you can take this time to do quick mindfulness meditation, breathing exercises, or simply go for a walk. Mindfulness meditation can help you bring your awareness to the present and notice your surroundings, which then takes you away from all the worries running through your mind. Breathing exercises are very useful in not only calming your body down but also helps you stay focused by practicing your breathing patterns. If you may not have the privacy or opportunity to do those things, you can opt to just go for a walk. However, keep in mind that you should not be speeding through the process on this walk. Try to incorporating mindfulness by focusing on the things around you, such as the people, noise, smells, and buildings. Pay attention to what's around you and try to see if you notice things around you that you've never noticed before. Taking these timeouts every day will help give your mind a break from the constant worrying and give you the opportunity to focus on the present.

- **Exercise #2: Opting for healthy meals**

Think about how your mind and your body are very connected. If you worry, you begin to feel the emotion of anxiety; if you experience this emotion for too long, you begin showing physical symptoms. By improving your physical health, it can work in reverse, where putting the right nutrients and vitamins into your body can help your mind feel healthier too.

Research has proven that making healthier changes in an individual's diet can make substantial changes in one's general mood or sense of well-being. Although it is not a complete substitute treatment, it is a great way to complement whatever treatments an individual is taking to reduce anxiety, stress, and depression. Here are a few tips that you can take to achieve a more well-balanced diet.

- Include some protein in your breakfast. Having protein at breakfast helps many people feel fuller and for longer. It helps keep blood sugar steady and helps give you more energy at the beginning of the day.

- Opt for complex carbohydrates. Research has found evidence that carbohydrates increase serotonin amount in the brain, which produces a calming effect. Opt for foods that are rich in complex carbs such as quinoa, oatmeal, whole-grain cereals, and whole-grain bread. Try to avoid foods that contain simple carbohydrates like sugary drinks and foods.

- Increase your water consumption. Even the mildest dehydration can cause symptoms like irritability and dry mouth, which is enough to negatively affect a person's mood.

If you are someone that's been experiencing a lot of anxiety, being mindful of what you are eating can help mitigate some of those feelings. Some of the newest research suggests that specific foods can help reduce anxiety based on the nutrients they bring. Here is a list of suggested foods and how they can help reduce anxiety:

- Brazil Nuts: This type of nut is high in the element selenium. Selenium is proven to improve mood because it reduces inflammation, which is often at increased levels if someone is suffering from an anxiety or mood disorder. Certain soybeans, mushrooms, and nut products are also a good source of selenium. Keep in mind to not consume too much selenium has there can be side effects. The recommended limit for adults is 400 mcg per day.

- Fatty Fish: Trout, salmon, sardines, herring, and mackerel are all fish that are high in omega-3. Omega-3 is a fatty acid that has been proven recently to have a strong link with improving cognitive function and mental health. Foods that contain lots of Omega-3 provides two essential fatty acids, EPA and DHA. EPA and DHA are great at reducing inflammation and promotes healthy brain function.

- Vitamin D: Much research tinks vitamin D deficiency to disorders like anxiety and depression. There has been enough evidence over the years to prove that vitamin D improves depression and anxiety. You can also use it to improve other disorders like seasonal disaffected disorder during winter times.

- Eggs: Egg yolks contain a lot of vitamin D and are also a great source of protein. Since it is a complete protein, it contains the necessary amino acids for your body's growth and development. Eggs also contain an amino acid called tryptophan, which aids in the creation of serotonin.

- Pumpkin Seeds: Pumpkin seeds are a superb source of potassium, which is responsible for regulating electrolytes and managing blood pressure. Potassium-rich foods are proven to reduce symptoms of anxiety and stress.

- Dark chocolate: Dark chocolate is an excellent source of magnesium. Magnesium has been proven to reduce symptoms of depression and anxiety. Dark chocolate is also high in tryptophan, which helps with serotonin production.

- Turmeric: Turmeric contains an active ingredient called curcumin, which lowers anxiety from its inflammation-reducing ability.

- Chamomile: Chamomile has properties of anti-inflammation, antioxidant, antibacterial, and relaxant. Chamomile has been proven to reduce various anxiety symptoms.

- Yogurt: Yogurt contains many healthy bacteria that have been proven to have positive effects on the health of the brain. Due to its anti-inflammatory effects, yogurt has been proven to reduce the inflammation that is partially responsible for depression, stress, and anxiety.

- Green Tea: Green tea contains theanine, which is a type of amino acid. It has calming and anti-anxiety effects and promotes the production of serotonin and dopamine.

- **Exercise #3: Avoid anxiety-inducing foods**

Just like how many foods aid in reducing inflammation that has been proved to be linked to enhancing symptoms of anxiety, other foods do the opposite. Moreover, foods that contain high sugars can lead to a feeling of jitteriness or hyperactivity. Like caffeine, high sugars can emphasize anxiety symptoms, which can make an individual feel worse. Here are a few foods that you should try to avoid to manage your anxiety symptoms:

- Fruit Juice: Fruit juice is mostly sugar water that works quickly to make you feel hyper but will bring you down just as fast. It often leaves people feeling hungry, which worsens symptoms of anxiety. Try to opt for whole food instead because the fiber works well to fill you up and slows down the intake of energy into your blood, which events the feeling of hyperactivity.

- Soda: Similar to fruit juice, soda contains a ton of sugar, which will cause a similar hyper to crash effect as fruit juice. Research has proven that sugary drinks have a direct link to anxiety and depression. Try to opt for soda water with a splash of juice to satisfy the craving without consuming the sugar.

- White Bread: White bread is made from highly processed white flour that turns into blood sugar when you eat it. It causes energy spikes and crashes that emphasize the symptoms of anxiety and depression. Opt for whole-grain bread (not whole wheat as sometimes it is just white bread dyed brown).

- Salad Dressing: Pre-packed salad dressing often contains a ton of sugar due to the use of high fructose corn syrup. This can also cause energy spikes and crashes.

- Ketchup: Ketchup is made of mostly sugar and can lead to an energy spike and crash. Even ketchup that is advertised as 'light' contains artificial sweeteners that have been proven to be linked to depression and anxiety. Opt for homemade salsa instead to limit the sugar intake.

- Processed Foods: Processed foods contain a lot of sugar or other preservatives that have been related to enhancing the symptoms of anxiety and depression. This includes refined cereals, fried foods, pastries, candy, and high-fat dairy products.

- **Exercise #4: Avoid caffeine and alcohol**

Caffeine is a stimulant that gives someone jittery effects similar to the feelings of those experiencing a frightening event. Caffeine actually triggers our natural flight or fight response and can make existing anxiety worse or, in serious cases, trigger a panic attack. Moreover, having too much caffeine can even make a non-anxious person feel nervous or moody. Anxiety is mindfulness's worst enemy; with anxious feelings present, it is difficult to be mindful of the present.

Alcohol has always been strongly linked to anxiety. Lots of research has proven that individuals who suffer from anxiety disorders are 2-3 times more likely to have problems with drugs or alcohol. Opposite from caffeine, alcohol is a depressant and can make certain symptoms of anxiety feel even worse. Many people with anxiety disorders turn to alcohol as self-treatment because of its immediate calming effects. However, as your body begins to process this alcohol, it often makes people feel edgy and commonly interferes with sleep. Moreover, alcohol dehydrates a person's body significantly, which creates symptoms of dehydration, which are similar to the symptoms of anxiety. It can also cause hangovers, which can further debilitate someone who is suffering from a mental disorder. Long story short, if you are someone who is suffering from a mental disorder, cutting out alcohol is a good first step.

- **Exercise #5: Do more physical exercise**

Although most people relate physical exercise to improve physical health, many studies have proven that exercise is absolutely necessary for maintaining mental health. Exercise helps to reduce stress, fatigue and improves concentration and overall cognitive function. This is particularly helpful when stress has depleted an individual's overall energy or ability to concentrate. Biologically, when stress begins to affect one's brain, the nerve connections affect the rest of the body to feel that impact as well. Vice versa, when your body feels better, your mind does too. Exercise helps your body produce endorphins (your body's natural painkillers) and improves the ability and quality of sleep, which then helps reduce stress.

Psychologists that have studied the relationship between exercise and anxiety suggest that a 10-minute walk every day can be as good as a 45-minute workout. Other studies showed that exercise works quickly and can help improve a depressed or anxious person's mood. The effects may be temporary, but a brisk walk or a simple workout can provide hours of relief. More research has shown that physically active individuals have lower anxiety and depression rates than sedentary people.

- **Exercise #6: Improving your sleep cycle**

If an individual is experiencing stress, worry, or anxiety, they have a very chance of struggling to achieve a healthy sleep cycle. They may have trouble falling asleep or staying asleep during the night. A vigorous mental activity like worrying tends to keep the brain from settling down, which causes the inability to fall asleep or stay asleep. Lack of sleep then causes an individual to feel more on edge the next day.

There are a few ways of how an individual can tackle their sleep problems. First, they can incorporate exercise to tire the body out and clear the mind of mental activity. They can also try to improve their diet, which leads to a better balance of nutrition that can aid with improving sleep quality. Here are a few tips on how to improve sleep to manage anxiety:

- Exercise: Exercise has been directly linked to lower symptoms of anxiety and sleep improvement. It can help readjust your sleeping cycle and can treat illnesses like insomnia or sleep apnea.

- Tailor Your Environment: Different people have different requirements of how they prefer their sleeping environment. Controlling things like temperature, sound, and light can help people get a good night's rest. The majority of people find that keeping the bedroom darker, cooler, and quieter helps achieve a better night's sleep.

- Avoiding Caffeine and Alcohol: As we mentioned previously, caffeine causes jitteriness, which can get in the way of falling or staying asleep. Alcohol also increases the heart rate, which is a culprit in keeping people awake. Instead of drinking caffeine and alcohol often, try drinking plain water to stay hydrated to promote healthier sleep.

- Calming Your Mind: Limiting the amount of mental activity in your brain before sleep can help improve the time it takes you to fall asleep and the actual sleep quality. Try some relaxation techniques like mindfulness or breathing exercises as you go to bed to keep your mind calm. Practicing these techniques in the day also helps you apply them easier at night.

- Limiting Screen Time: The light that emits from our electronics keeps our minds awake, which is detrimental when you are trying to fall asleep. Try to limit your screen time before you go to bed. Things like checking work emails or social media can trigger worries and stress that will keep your mind active all night.

An unhealthy sleeping schedule can cause a person a lot of anxiety, which will slow down or even prevent their process of achieving mindfulness. Improving your overall sleep cycle will keep your mind fresh and decrease the risk of generating anxious thoughts.

- **Exercise #7: Socialize**

Humans are innately a social species. Throughout our generations, being social has helped humans thrive and survive. One of the reasons for this is that humans are innately compassionate living beings, and we need to satisfy that in order to feel fulfilled. When you take away socialization, humans naturally tend to feel unfulfilled and lonely. By making an effort to go out into the world and be around others, people can begin to feel like they are apart of society. Social activities decrease the feeling of loneliness while promoting those of enjoyment, belonging, security, and safety.

Socialization is proven to directly impact our anxiety and stress levels in several ways. First, socialization promotes a hormone responsible for decreasing anxiety levels and makes us feel more confident in our ability to cope with anxiety and stress. It also encourages us to spend our energy outwards rather than inwards. Often, when people are focused on reaching out to others, they are distracted from their own stress, pain, or circumstances. When people spend time socializing, they actually strengthen their sense of 'life has meaning and purpose' and ultimately increases their mood. Here are a few things you can do to try to increase your socialization:

- Initiate social interactions with friends or family. Do things like talk on the phone, eat at a restaurant, have a party, or even exercise together.
- Introduce yourself to people you come in contact with often, like your neighbors.
- Join classes or groups that interest you (exercise groups, hobby groups, etc.)

Do bear in mind that it is quality socialization that counts rather than quantity. If you surround yourself with a large number of people that you don't know that well is not as effective as surrounding yourself with 2 - 3 close friends/family to socialize with.

- **Exercise #8: Improving your bad habits**

Let's start with improving procrastination habits. Individuals procrastinate for numerous reasons, but the main goal is to achieve a temporary sense of relief. The problem here is that the relief is temporary and is quickly replaced with the anxiety about being behind on the things you need to get done. If you are suffering from an anxiety disorder, you probably procrastinate out of failure or fear of disapproval. People often put off phone calls, discussing issues at work, or scheduling needed appointments. By procrastinating, you are not paying attention to the present, and you are actually giving your brain things to think about that aren't of the present moment. Here are three tips to help you begin to deal with procrastination:

- Make a list of tasks that prioritizes the things that need to be done.
- Reward yourself for completing difficult tasks.
- Use relaxation strategies to help deal with the anxiety about completing certain tasks.

Next, let's discuss how internet usage, cell phone usage, and social media can create more anxiety and stress. When almost everything we do nowadays is held on the internet, it is hard to stay away from it. The news is on the internet; your work emails, work schedule, entertainment, and even your money are on the internet! Many people have developed a dependence on technology and find it hard to do other meaningful things like socializing face to face. Technology and the internet constantly allow us to avoid things like face-to-face contact, making people more afraid of it. Social media is a major culprit in creating unrealistic expectations of many things that range from physical looks to extreme lifestyles. People who are active on social media can't help but compare their 'regular' lives to extravagant ones on the internet, which leads to anxiety regarding their own accomplishments and successes. This will cause you to become less mindful of your own presence and become immersed in other people's lives.

Improving your internet, cellphone, and social media usage can help you get a better grip of reality and help you differentiate yourself from others. Firstly, start by trying to reduce the amount of time you spend on social media and on the internet. Reducing the amount of time and energy you dedicate to this will give you more time and energy to do other things out in the world. Secondly, take everything you see on social media and the internet with a grain of salt. Just because your childhood friend is posting tons of pictures of their new Ferrari does not necessarily mean they have their life together. Don't believe everything you see, and make sure to fact-check certain articles or posts on social media.

Chapter 6: Mindfulness for Stress and Anxiety During Covid-19

As I mentioned earlier, due to our increasingly stressful and busy lives - more and more people face health problems such as depression and anxiety, especially due to the uncertainty and global turmoil brought about by the year 2020. Many doctors who specialize in the area of mental health have begun to study and even practice meditation and mindfulness techniques to promote a healthier brain and mind, and in this chapter, we will look at how mindfulness can be used to combat stress and anxiety specifically.

The three most common reasons why a person seeks a meditation and mindfulness practice are anxiety, depression, and stress. Let's learn a little bit more about these different types of struggles and what they look like, and how meditation and mindfulness will help you to combat them.

How Meditation and Mindfulness Can Help Reduce Stress and Anxiety in Uncertain Times

One of the most common reasons that people decide to practice mindfulness is to become more in tune with their emotions and feelings. This is especially true for people who may be suffering from feelings like stress, anxiety, or depression. If someone is diagnosed with a mental disorder, professionals regularly advise them to practice and improve their mindfulness. In this chapter, I will be teaching you how to become more mindful of your own emotions, feelings, and thoughts. This is actually a huge component of Cognitive Behavioral Therapy. CBT is a type of speaking therapy currently ranked as the most effective form of treatment for people with mental disorders. I will be teaching you about some exercises from this program that you can use to help you become more mindful of your thoughts and emotions, challenge negative ones, and change your negative thinking into healthy thinking.

Mindfulness for Anxiety

Did you know that anxiety disorders are the most common mental illness in the United States? There are a variety of different anxiety disorders. Still, most of the time, when people use the word *anxiety*, they are referring to the most common type of anxiety, "generalized anxiety disorder." This disorder affects 40 million adults worldwide, so you are not alone if this is your reason for reading this book!

Interestingly, humans have experienced anxiety since the beginning of time. Back in those days, anxiety helped protect us from dangerous situations, such as predators or a lack of food. Anxiety is a basic emotion that all species experience.

The feeling of anxiety is what triggers the fight or flight response, which you may have heard of. The fight or flight response is the feeling that you get when you must make a quick decision about whether to fight for your life or run for your life.

This is by no means a pleasant feeling or experience, but it is not a dangerous one. In fact, anxiety is extremely helpful to most living beings, such as animals that hunt for their food or that must flee from predators.

Although we no longer have the actual need for the fight or flight response in modern-day society, this function is still ingrained within our brains, and it is impossible to remove it from our nature. In modern-day societies, anxiety has become a huge problem, and instead of helping us survive and live, it is actually negatively affecting many people's lives.

If the description of anxiety is something you relate to and think you struggle with, mindfulness and meditation can help you ease and improve many of its symptoms. Take a look at the most commonly reported symptoms of anxiety:

- **Excessive Worrying**

Worrying is the most common 'symptom' of anxiety. However, worry is more often seen as the cause of anxiety, which then produces more worry. This results in a vicious cycle of worry and anxiety.

Worry often occurs in normal daily situations. For an individual to be officially diagnosed with anxiety, worrying has to occur almost every day for a minimum of six months. Further, the person must have difficulty in controlling their worry.

If this sounds like something you experience, you likely suffer from anxiety. Fear not, the rest of this book is going to help you find ways to combat this!

- **Restlessness**

Another common symptom of anxiety is restlessness. This is primarily dominant in teenagers and children. The feeling of restlessness is often described as having an uncomfortable urge to constantly move the body or feeling 'on edge.'

This is often showcased in the form of tapping your fingers or fidgeting with something. A recent study of children diagnosed with anxiety found that over 70% suffered from restlessness as their main symptom of anxiety. Although restlessness is not a symptom in everybody who experiences anxiety, it is one of the first major symptoms that doctors look for when making a diagnosis.

- **Excessive Agitation**

Biologically, when somebody is feeling anxious, their nervous system begins to go into overdrive. This kicks off a series of effects throughout the human body. Symptoms of agitation can include a racing heart, shaky hands, dry mouth, and sweaty palms. When your brain senses danger, it begins to prepare your body to react to the danger, which leads to the symptoms above. This is in preparation for the "fight or flight" response, as we discussed at the beginning of this chapter.

Although this is extremely helpful in the presence of a real threat, it is debilitating in the modern-day, as most of our worries are not physical threats.

- **Insomnia**

Sleep disturbances such as trouble falling asleep or staying asleep are strongly associated with anxiety disorders. This is likely due to the worrying and thinking in an anxious person's head.

Similar to many symptoms above, it is unclear whether insomnia contributes to anxiety or if anxiety contributes to insomnia. However, it is proven that once an anxiety disorder has been properly treated, insomnia often improves as well. This is due to the strong relationship between anxiety and insomnia.

Suppose this is something that you are suffering from. In that case, you are likely happy to learn that treating your anxiety using mindfulness and meditation will also help you to begin sleeping through the night and feeling more rested in the morning!

Mindfulness for Dealing With Depression

The second reason that many people seek help in the form of meditation and mindfulness is depression.

Depression is an illness that is often discussed, but do you know what depression really is?

A person can feel "depressed" as an emotion, but this does not necessarily mean that they can be diagnosed with depression. Firstly, depression is a serious and very common mental illness that negatively affects the way people feel.

Since depression heavily affects how a person feels, it also affects the way they think and how they act. Luckily, depression is a treatable illness, and it is something that can be recovered from using the right treatments, such as meditation and mindfulness.

Depression typically causes a person to feel sadness and is often found along with a loss of interest in most activities, especially those that once brought them joy. It can also lead to a multitude of emotional and physical problems. It can hinder a person's ability to live their daily life, including hindering their regular functioning at work or in the home.

Why is there an epidemic of depression in recent times? It's almost as if every time we turn a corner, we meet someone who is suffering from depression and/or anxiety. Is the reason for this simply because mental illness is being discussed today more than ever? Or is it because more and more people are being diagnosed with depression?

Mental health experts are focused on researching these questions, but the most important thing at this point is treating your depression. After looking at the most common symptoms of depression, we will look at how mindfulness and meditation can help you deal with it.

Mindfulness and meditation have been proven to help improve the symptoms of depression. If you feel like this is a struggle that you are currently facing, ensuring that you understand the most common symptoms of depression will help you to determine which symptoms you are dealing with and which symptoms you want to rid yourself of.

- **Constant Sadness**

This symptom is the feeling of sadness that occurs in a depressed person for no apparent reason. This feeling can feel very intense; it often feels like nothing can make it go away.

- **Suicidal or dark thoughts**

These types of thoughts can occur very frequently during a person's depression. These thoughts have to be taken very seriously, and when a person is experiencing these emotions, they must ask for help right away.

- **Feeling of worthlessness**

A person that is depressed often experiences unrealistic feelings of worthlessness or guilt. Usually, there isn't a specific event that provokes these feelings; they just happen at random.

- **Loss of interest or pleasure in activities that were previously enjoyed**

A person that is depressed may experience a loss of interest that affects all areas of their life. This can range from not finding pleasure from their previous hobbies to everyday activities that the person used to enjoy.

- **Low energy**

People who have depression typically always feel low on energy even if they have not exerted themselves. This type of depressive fatigue is different because neither sleep nor rest can alleviate this tiredness.

- **Impression of restlessness**

For some people, depression makes them very jumpy and agitated. They may struggle with sitting still and fiddling with items.

- **Aches and pain**

Depression can often cause physical pain. This includes joint pain, stomach pain, headaches, back pain, or other pains).

- **Psychomotor impairment**

Depression can make a person feel as if everything is slowed down. This includes slowed speech, body movement, thinking, speech that is in low volume, long pauses before answering, inflection or muteness.

Mindfulness Techniques for Managing Anxiety and Depression

Now that you understand the most common symptoms of anxiety, depression, and chronic stress and have pinpointed the symptoms that you experience, we will look at how you can use meditation and mindfulness to deal with these symptoms.

As you can see above, many of the symptoms of these mental health disorders are similar. If you are experiencing symptoms like insomnia, it could result from one or several mental health issues. Upon reading this chapter, I hope you have gained a better understanding of your symptoms' root causes. Even if you are unsure, you can begin to deal with your symptoms using meditation and mindfulness, leading to a healthier and happier life overall.

When treating anxiety, depression, or chronic stress using meditation and mindfulness, there are a few steps that you can follow, especially in the instance of an acute anxiety attack or depressive episode. Below, you can see the steps you can take to employ mindfulness in these situations, along with an example of how they can be used to manage these situations before and during they occur.

Mindfulness and meditation are great ways to reduce your stress levels and get in touch with your body and its sensations. Mindfulness focuses on bringing your consciousness to the present moment and focusing on your body, its sensations, the sounds it hears, and what it feels like from the inside. Mindfulness involves noticing the thoughts that come into your mind and letting them pass by, not paying them too much attention. Mindfulness is a great practice for those who have difficulty getting out of their heads and tend to think quite a bit. Mindfulness can be used for various reasons, but here we will focus on its use for reducing stress and anxiety and getting in touch with your body on a physical level. Mindfulness and meditation go hand in hand. Meditation increases mindfulness while mindfulness improves and deepens meditation. Meditation is a practice, while mindfulness is a state of being.

To get into a state of mindfulness involves getting quiet and observing, without judgment, everything that occurs within your body. You must let your thoughts drift by, noticing but not judging them. Pay attention to the sensations in your body. Is there tightness or tension anywhere? Notice your chest rising /falling with each breath and the weight of your body on the chair or bed. Notice also your emotions and feelings. By doing this repeatedly, you will be able to eventually focus on your body with less and less distracting thoughts. When your thoughts start to distract you, bring your attention back to your body and your breathing. Being able to reach a state like this allows you to reconnect with your body from the inside and is beneficial for reducing your anxiety and stress levels.

Being able to reach a state like this allows you to reconnect with your body from the inside. Approaching your body with a non-judgment mindset will also make it easier for you to change your beliefs about your body or introduce new thoughts and behaviors. Instead of letting your mind spiral with anxious *what-if* thoughts, you will not let them escalate. They will not escalate to the level they normally would because instead of judging yourself and your body and worrying about what is wrong with you, you will approach it as is and without trying to force anything.

By trying this exercise several times, it will begin to come easier over time, and you will then be able to get into a state of self-hypnosis much quicker. Once you have reached this level, you can then practice any sort of hypnosis in the form of self-hypnotism.

Mindfulness for Dealing With Panic Attacks

Panic attacks or anxiety attacks are commonly associated with anxiety. Panic attacks are actually their own form of an anxiety disorder, known as Panic Disorder.

To put it simply, panic attacks are when an individual is feeling an overwhelming, intense sensation of fear that can be completely debilitating. This fear comes with the symptoms of a racing heart, shakiness, sweating, fear of dying, chest tightness, and shortness of breath.

Panic attacks can happen in public places or if you are by yourself. If individuals find that they have panic attacks frequently and unexpectedly, they are likely suffering from a panic disorder. A shocking statistic of 22% of adults in the population has experienced panic attacks at some point in their life. However, only 3% meet the criteria for a panic disorder.

Mindfulness and meditation are proven to be effective solutions for people suffering from Panic Disorder. If this is something that you are struggling with, this subchapter will give you some tangible strategies for dealing with them before and as they come up!

1. Make a Plan Before any Panic Attacks Happen.

Regardless of what plan you have made for yourself, having one ready to go is extremely important. Try to think about this plan like an instruction list that you will follow if you have a panic attack building. This may include getting out of the current situation, lying down, or panic attacks, or anxiety attacks are commonly associated with anxiety. Panic attacks are actually their own form of an anxiety disorder; this is known as Panic Disorder. To put it simply, panic attacks are when an individual is feeling an overwhelming, intense sensation of fear that can be completely debilitating. This fear comes with the symptoms of a racing heart, shakiness, sweating, fear of dying, chest tightness, and shortness of breath. Panic attacks can happen in public places or if you are by yourself. If individuals find that they have panic attacks frequently and unexpectedly, they are likely suffering from a panic disorder. A shocking statistic of 22% of adults in the population has experienced panic attacks at some point in their life. However, only 3% meet the criteria for a panic disorder. Calling your friends to distract yourself from the building anxiety and to help you relax.

By getting yourself out of that current situation, you can start the next steps in this list:

2. Employ Breathing Deeply Regularly.

Since feeling short on breath and oxygen is one of the symptoms of a panic attack, practicing deep breathing could help alleviate it. Having shortness of breath is also one of the main contributors to the feelings of franticness and lack of control. Make sure you are acknowledging that the short breathing is associated with your panic attack and that it is likely not due to a medical condition, nor is it permanent.

Next, take a deep breath that lasts at least 4 seconds. Hold it for 1 second, then let it go for another 4 seconds. Repeat the cycle of breathing until you gain control and are breathing steadier. Focus on simply counting to four when breathing, which will prevent hyperventilation and distract other symptoms from occurring.

3. Practice Muscle Relaxation.

If you are in the midst of a panic attack, you will likely feel as though your body control is completely gone. Using relaxation techniques for your muscles will help you regain control to some level. "Progressive muscle relaxation" is the name for a great technique at helping to alleviate symptoms of anxiety and panic disorders.

The first step is to start clenching your fists and holding the clench for 10 seconds. When you reach ten, let go of your clench, relax the hands entirely. Then, do this again but with the feet and progressively do this along your body by tightening and releasing every section of the body. This includes the midsection, glutes, legs, arms, face, neck, and shoulders.

4. Choose a Mantra and Repeat it Regularly.

This technique often sounds a little cheesy or awkward, but it is a great coping technique specific to panic disorders. Telling yourself a mantra while having a panic attack is one good way to center yourself back in the moment. Try repeating simple positive and encouraging phrases like "This is just a temporary feeling." or "I am okay, I will be okay." or "I'm not going to die. I just need to focus on my breathing."

5. Focus on an Object Near you.

This technique begins by picking an object that is in the area you are in. Take note of everything you notice about this specific object. For example, focus on the color, size, or any patterns that this object may have. Think about where you have seen other objects like this or what other objects look similar to this. You can either think about this silently or say it out loud as if you are talking to someone. This technique helps you bring your attention away from the feelings of a panic attack and into your surroundings. By refocusing your attention, you should be able to decrease the severity of the panic attack.

Chapter 7: Mindfulness Exercise Workbook

To help improve mindfulness, we must be able to show ourselves the love we need. Sometimes, our thoughts naturally drift to a place where we become consumed by feelings of worthlessness and dread. When our minds are filled with negative thoughts, we are preoccupying our minds with everything that can go wrong. We don't pay attention to the things that are actually happening at the moment. Practicing a more positive thinking pattern will leave more room in your mind to be mindful. The exercises in this chapter will help you love yourself more to stop these negative thoughts, in turn allowing you more mental space to be mindful.

Self-Compassion Worksheet

In this exercise, we will be focusing on improving your understanding of yourself and the love you have for yourself. This exercise just requires a few minutes of your day where you focus on showing yourself compassion.

Those who enjoy writing or prefer to express themselves through the use of words will find this exercise very helpful. This worksheet is set up into three segments and is also effective for people who aren't writers.

Follow these directions below:

Part 1:

Start by thinking about all the weaknesses you have that cause you to feel inferior. Everybody has various things that they may not like about themselves or makes them feel unequal.

Next, think about things that make you insecure. If there is one particular item that stands out to you, bring it to the forefront of your mind.

Pay attention to your feelings when focusing on your insecurity. Notice what emotions and feelings arise and let yourself experience them. People often disallow themselves to feel negative emotions, but these are all important parts of life. Negative feelings can also bring out positive outcomes such as self-acceptance.

Simply feel those emotions that arise while thinking about your insecurities. Write a blurb on the emotions that you feel:

____

____

____

____

____

____

Part 2:

Now that you have written about your emotions, you can begin the second part of this exercise. In this exercise, you will be writing a letter to yourself from the perspective of a sympathetic loved one or imaginary friend.

The purpose of this exercise is to show you the compassion and understanding that you often show to your friends, to yourself.

Start this exercise by imagining a friend who is a compassionate, kind, accepting, and unconditionally loving person. Then, imagine that they share the same strengths and weaknesses as you.

Think about how this friend would think about you. They love you, they are kind to you, and they accept you. Even if you have done something to hurt their feelings, this friend is understanding and is quick to forgive.

Your friend is understanding and sympathetic, but they also know everything about your life. They know every decision that you've made to get to where you are, each step that you took in your journey, and they acknowledge all the factors that have played a role in who you are today.

Next, write a letter to yourself from the perspective of your imaginary friend. Tailor the body of this letter on the insecurities that you have written down in part one. Think about the things this friend would say to you.

Will they tell you that your mistakes and weaknesses are unacceptable? Will they tell you that you need to be perfect? Or will they tell you that they sympathize with all the feelings you are going through?

Would they be mad at you if you feel inadequate or insecure? Will they happily encourage you to accept everything about yourself? Will they remind you of your positive traits and your strengths?

Write this letter in their perspective and make sure you are showcasing themes of kindness, compassion, and love.

Dear _________,

____

____

____

____

____

____

____

____

____

____

____

____

____

____

____

____

____

____

____

____

____

____

____

____

Sincerely,

____

Part 3:
When you complete this letter, take a short break and give yourself some space away from this exercise.

When you are ready to come back, read the letter you wrote with the intention to really take in what it's saying. Don't just read it as something you wrote for yourself but read it as if it really were from a friend.

Open yourself up to the sympathy and compassion that your friend is showing you. Let those words comfort and soothe you. Let those words sink in and have it turn into compassion for yourself.

Compassion Therapy Worksheet

The following worksheet is more of a guide than an exercise. This guide is here to help you learn about compassion focused therapy and how it can play an important role in our lives. This is something you want to read if you are someone who is having difficulty expressing compassion to yourself.

Let's start by learning some of the background information on CFT:

- CFT was developed to help manage feelings of self-loathing, criticism, and shame.
- CFT is useful when treating mental illnesses or other related problems.
- CFT is founded on a new model that was built from the science that backs human nature, attachment, and evolution.

Now, let's talk about how evolution has shaped the human brain.

- There are three layers in our brain, each being more modern than the last:
    - Reptilian Brain: The oldest and most basic part of our brain, its focuses are survival, territory, food, and temperature.
    - Mammalian brain: The next level up from the reptilian brain, it is focused on living with groups, nurturing, status, and hierarchy.
    - Human brain: This is the most modern development of the brain and is focused on caregiving, relationship forming, and higher-order thinking.

The CFT model is explained by the following:

- The CFT model proposes that humans use three systems to manage their emotions:
  - Threat System: The motivation behind this system is to survive, and its attention is focused on the fight or flight mindset, threat, fear, anxiety, and danger.
  - Drive system: The motivation behind this system is to win, and its focus is on goals and finding an advantage.
  - Caregiving system: The motivation behind this system is to look after and soothe another; its main focus is other's distress or pain.
  - Everyone is born with all these systems ready to go. Depending on our environment, it determines which systems are used.

Since compassion helps manage the symptoms of mental illness:

- The goal of CFT is to help people utilize and further develop their caregiving system. This is what will help them come to terms with their thoughts and feel comfortable in their own bodies.
- The caregiving system aids in activating warmth, empathy, strength, kindness, non-judgment, wisdom, and moral courage.
- The practice of CFT is divided into three parts:
  - Learning the skills needed to develop the caregiving system
  - Learning about human nature

o   Practice activating the caregiving system and implementing it in daily life

Here are some key messages to keep in mind:
- "The bad things that have happened in your life are not your fault. However, you will be the one that is responsible for alleviating your own suffering."
- "Compassion is all about choosing to be the best version of yourself."

Next, we are going to learn about the process of forming compassion for yourself. Don't be intimidated, although it seems like a hard process because of how deeply out self-criticism is embedded within us and how long it's been there.

The CFT follows this format "Problem > Coping Strategy > Unintended Consequences". It focuses on the importance of compassion.

The first step here is to figure out all the past influences that lead you to feel self-criticism and shame in the present day. This step here helps you acknowledge these shameful memories or past trauma that may have manifested into shame.

In the space below, write down the fears you struggle with the most. Give attention to the feelings of blame, criticism, and shame. Keep in mind that there are two types of fear, internal and external. Internal fears are like depression, anxiety, rage, shame, and external fears when someone hurts your feelings.

____

____

____

____

____

Next, write down some defensive measures that you have in place to avoid getting hurt or to lower the risk of getting hurt. This could be avoiding social contact altogether as a way to prevent rejection.

____

____

____

____

____

People often use internal defensive behaviors to keep themselves from feeling those difficult emotions or problems. This includes things like dissociating, substance abuse, self-harm, or a constant reminder of weaknesses. External behaviors are used to avoid being harmed by other people. This includes being silent, submissive, and keeping a distance from other people.

In the last exercise here, we will learn about the effects of the cycle of safety and defensive behaviors related to unintended consequences. These consequences are the outcomes from the safety behaviors that a person exhibits, although they may not be intending to produce them. These consequences can be self harassment or emotional isolation. In the space below, write down what sort of safety behavior you think you have and write down whether you think it harms you or protects you.

____

____

____

____

____

These unintended consequences likely have a large impact on how you understand yourself. People may attack themselves for exhibiting these unintended consequences, which may spiral into even more unhealthy defensive behaviors. This cycle tends to feed on itself.

This worksheet is often emotionally difficult to complete because you have to dig deep and find out that you haven't shown yourself enough compassion. This is an important step for those working on their compassion and self-acceptance to identify these bad behaviors and begin to change them.

Conclusion

The most important and crucial aspect of your success in meditation is how you prepare for it. Without any preparation, meditation can feel clumsy, ineffective, and may even feel like a chore. That is not what we want to get out of your meditation journey. Let's begin to discuss how you can prepare for meditation to prevent an unsatisfying experience. We are going to close this chapter by discussing the obstacles that you may face with meditation.

Despite the many benefits of meditation, many people, especially beginners, stop meditating when confronted with obstacles in their practice. It's hard to blame them because meditation looks deceivingly simple. How hard can it be to sit down and seemingly be doing nothing at all? Well, meditation is far from doing nothing at all. It is an active training of the mind to increase its strength. This, in turn, increases mindfulness, concentration, and resiliency. Unfortunately, these qualities are hard to come by in our instant culture. This type of meditation training requires both effort and commitment. It also requires a lot of time to put in if you want to transform and strengthen your mind.

I want all new meditators to realize that overcoming problems within our meditation practice is also part of the practice itself. If you can work past the obstacles that stop you from practicing, our minds become more resilient and focused despite the external and internal influences.

To end this book, I have provided you with the most commonly-asked questions by beginners and the answers to these questions. Happy meditating!

Frequently-Asked Questions

How Long Will it Take to See Results?

Some people have found that meditation brings about numerous benefits immediately, whereas others have found that it has taken more practice and time to achieve those benefits. As I mentioned earlier in this book, meditation affects you by strengthening your mind and allowing you to control and influence the thoughts that go through it.

Having a strong mind and awareness is said to help achieve your inner peace. Meditation every day is like a workout for your brain. Think of it as something physical, like looking to gain 10 pounds of muscle in the gym. The first few sessions of your workout definitely won't be able to produce anything noticeable. However, you do feel the changes and effects of a workout almost immediately. The more you work out, the stronger and bigger your muscles get. This is exactly like meditation. The first few times you begin to meditate, you may not notice any changes to your stress levels or anxiety levels. However, you will feel the immediate effects of it, which is a sense of relaxation, no matter how little or strong. The more persistent you are with meditating, you will begin to notice the more long term effects. Due to an increase in mindfulness, you may find yourself having the ability to catch yourself when you begin to daydream or become anxious about something. You will be able to catch yourself in the act of these bad habits and bring your mind back to the present. In addition to that, because meditation brings your awareness to your present surroundings, you will begin to notice little details in life that you may have overlooked in the past. You may start to notice the details of your house plant, or the shape of the clouds, or even notice new details of your own body. Little things like this in life tend to bring us bubbles of joy throughout the day. Allow yourself to savor these moments. Throughout your journey of meditation, I hope that you will begin to achieve more tangible benefits such as; stress reduction, increased emotional health, and sleep improvement.

Why Won't my Mind Stop Racing?

The problem here is that you're supposed to be focused on your meditation, but your mind keeps wandering off to other more immediate thoughts! You may encounter this problem more frequently if you have the bad habit of incessant self-talk that seems to have something to say about everything. Even about your new meditation practice! As mentioned in one of the earlier methods in this chapter, breath counting is a very effective method to calm down your racing mind. In layman's terms, the meditator needs to count every breath cycle. One inhale followed by one exhale, one complete breath cycle. Continue to count to 10, and aim to count to 100. However, if you lose count - you have to reset and start from one again.

The way that these methods work is very simple. Keeping your mind occupied with a simple task like counting will have less tendency to wander. However, sometimes your mind can get so used to the counting method that it can count AND wander simultaneously. If this happens, it is time to change this method's rules to force your mind to relearn and readapt. You can change the way you count by counting backward (e.g., starting at 100 and counting down to 1). You can also count in even numbers (e.g., starting at two and counting to 200). Keep switching them up to stay one step ahead of your tricky mind.

What do I do if I Keep Nodding Off or Spacing Out?

Another common problem that meditators face is drowsiness or spacing out. It is easy to get confused and believe that this counts as real meditation because you feel calm and comfortable. A lot of people fall asleep during meditation. What's happening here is that the mind has slid into a state of mental numbness in which you are not entirely conscious. It is almost as if you are trapped in a thick fog that blinds your vision. Instead of lacking clear vision, in meditation, your mind is lacking mindfulness and alertness. It hinders your ability to focus sharply. If your meditation aims to gain better mental clarity, spacing out is an obstacle you have to overcome.

What you can do when you catch yourself nodding off is to insert more energy into your session. This can be done in a few different ways. If your posture starts to fall apart, correct it right away. Start by straightening your back, tilt your chin higher, or contract your abdominal muscles. If you begin to lose focus, or your focus seems to be hazy, simply bring your awareness back to your breathing to refresh your mind. If you are chanting a mantra, try raising your voice a bit higher or chanting at a slightly faster speed. If you begin to feel sleepy, you can stand up and do a walking meditation around the room. It is a good idea to meditate away from your bed to avoid the temptation of dozing off.

Why do I See Colours, Lights, or Visions?

The problem here is that some people see vivid colors, lights, or visions when their eyes or closed or during meditation. This can be a distraction you face if you do normally see those things. On the other hand, other meditators may feel troubled because they see none of those things! First of all, we have to understand that seeing colors, lights, or visions is not an indication of one's meditation skill. Many great meditators see visions, and many don't. The one thing in common they both have is razor-sharp concentration power that has achieved them great wisdom or high spiritual attainment. When you are meditating, it is important to drop all expectations and focus your mind on the present.

Why Can't I Relax?

You may be familiar with the following scenario: You've just arrived home after a long and highly stressful day at work. You automatically think that meditation may be helpful, so you get into your starting sitting position. However, no matter how hard you are trying to focus, your mind is racing off more than usual. This actually makes you even more stressed out, and you begin to wonder why you can't begin your meditation. It is highly difficult to meditate when your mind is agitated. In the case of someone who is highly stressed out and on the verge of a panic attack, it is very difficult to bring your mind back to the present. It's almost like a CPU that is clocked at 100%; there simply isn't room to rearrange your thoughts and awareness. When the mind is this caught up in its own world, it's difficult to focus on your breaths or the meditation at hand except for the current thoughts it's obsessed with. A strategy to get it out of this agitated state would be to dissipate the energy and calm it down by an external means. Exercising, listening to music, going out for a walk, or having a conversation with someone are ways to calm it down. Every beginner meditator should be armed with at least one reliable external means to turn to when they are in a state of high stress or anxiety. When you become more experienced in your meditation journey, your mind will become more resilient to stress, and the effects will be more moderate.